Digital Photography for Beginners

To make you a better photographer

Introduction

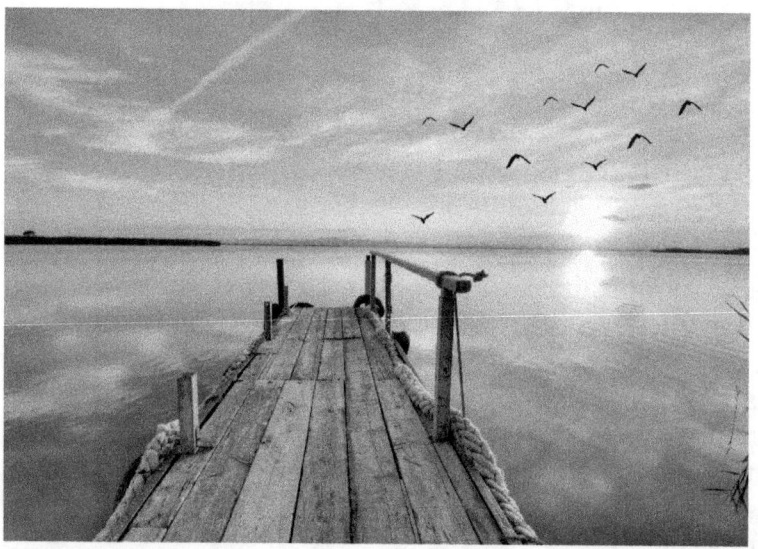

Most people love to look at and take great pictures. We all see creative shots we wish we would have taken. Because they tell a story, we can relate to. We also all like to share great photos with others.

The tough thing about being a great photographer is being able to capture with the camera what you see with your eyes. Training your eyes to see light and shadows and capture that image with your camera is the key. There is not a lens made that can capture the full range you can see with your eyes. The goal is to capture enough of what you see so you can share what you see with others.

To do that it takes a couple of key things. Number one is to know your camera like the back of your hand. The other is training yourself to see everything in the shot and set it up to tell a story with the image.

The only way to get to that point is to practice. Getting good at anything requires practice, photography is no different. The best way to practice is to get out and take pictures. It is hard to take creative pictures unless you have a plan. The key to a plan is to have projects, look for specific shots and concepts, to make great pictures.

This purpose of this book is to give you project ideas that will teach you what to see and what to look for. It will teach you things you can do to train yourself to become an accomplished photographer. Then you can make the shots you want.

I have taken several hundred thousand pictures over the past 30 years. I have taken many photography classes and went through the NYIP course back in the 1980s. My goal taking photos is always to get the finest shot I can. The projects in this book are ways I know will teach you to be the best photographer you can be with a little practice.

If you do these projects and focus on what you can learn from them, you will be a better photographer. You will get fantastic photos, and you will have fun doing it. The best time to get started is right now. You need not spend a lot of money and get new equipment right away. You can get great shots with any camera. Once you learn more, you will want to get better equipment, but you can start with your phone camera.

Think about how to do the projects. Then learn to look at things and plan of how to do them. You should know what you want to see and shoot when you practice. Go through the projects and spend time on each one. If you do, you will take the shots and people will look at them and say WOW.

Thank you for downloading and reading my book. Be willing to learn and you will improve your photography.

I would appreciate if you went to the Amazon site and leave a review of my book if you have a minute.

If you have comments or questions, you can contact me. mailto:steve@stevepease.net or visit stevepease.net for more great reads.

Have fun with the projects while you learn.

Table of Contents

23. <u>Framing</u>

Photo a day.

Most people think they can do this project. It sounds easy, but it is not. The issue becomes getting good subjects to shoot. You do not want to take snapshots. You want to learn as you take the shots and make great shots every day. Most of the photo a day challenges are for a year.

Many people start but do not finish the year. As long you focus on the project and learn, it is ok if you do not finish. Do it if you can. Learn to see light and shadows and learn to compose great shots. It is great if you finish, you will have a variety of great shots from throughout the year.

If you want to take a quality shot every day for an entire year, it will take time every day. It will also take planning and always looking for a shot and ideas for more shots. Start with a shorter goal. Try to do it for and month, if you are getting into it, try to keep up with it for a year. Starting with your phone camera is a great way to start. You always have the phone camera with you so you can get the shot when you see it.

You do not want to take a random snapshot every day, only to say you got your shot. To do this project right, you want to have quality photos at the end of the project for each day. It takes time on your part. You will have days when you cannot come up with anything to shoot. Not every day will be a great shot but try to make it a great shot.

This project will force you to use your creativity. You will learn to think about different things. Things like, how to take cool shots of ordinary things. Like a glass of water, a butter knife, a piece of fruit, etc. Take shots from different angles. Get down on the ground or up high. It is amazing how different things look from ground level. Take shots following the rules of photography, but also take shots that break the rules.

Take shots not lined up like they should be. Turn the camera at different angles and see what happens. Take shots lined up perfect as well. Use your imagination and have fun with it. **Here is a great website** where you can get tons of ideas. You can also see how many talented photographers work on challenges. I was into this site several years ago and had fun doing the challenges. Check it out.

Some days it is easy, we were at the lake, and I saw this shot and snapped it with my phone. This was a spontaneous shot, and you will get many of these. I have planned out shots also for
days. You will not always get great spontaneous shots.

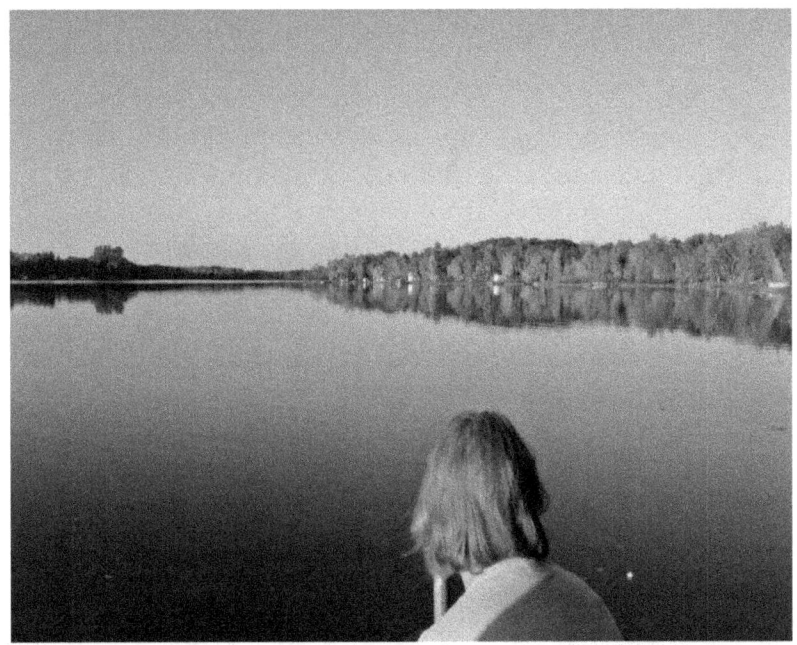

This picture tells a story about a beautiful evening sitting on the dock with a line in the water. The fall colors are changing and not a wave on the lake. The sun angle is low, close to sunset.

Very peaceful and relaxing, and it comes through in the shot. It brings back memories for me and my wife. However, anyone who was not there can still feel the peace and how nice it was when I took the shot.

Like I said before, this one was easy. Some days like this one; you will take 20 shots you feel would be a decent photo for your project. Other days when you work a full day, and you are gone most of the day, finding an acceptable shot can be a lot harder. Look all the time for good scenes and determine the best way to compose the shot.

To do it right, you need to take a unique shot every day. I know sometimes you are not able to do it, for whatever reason. You can cheat if you need to buy use a shot from a different day but only do it if you must. Try to get a good shot daily.

Lots of photographers think they can do this project. The challenge of this project is to do it every day for one yr. 365 days of photos. I have done this project many times. Sometimes for a couple of months, sometimes longer. I made it a whole year 1 time. It is always good practice to keep sharp in your skills.

Most people cannot keep up with it. It is a big commitment. You need to do it one day at a time, try it for a week, if you are having fun, go for a month and keep going if you want. The key is to get you to think about photography more and learn to see things in a different way.

One of the cool things about this project is you will think about photography all the time. Every day you are looking at things from a photography point of view. The project helps you see awesome photos all over the place. Places you have been often and things you see all the time, but you never saw it as a great photo before.

You can do the project and keep track of it on your own, but it is much more fun to do it on a website set up for it. Here is a link on Pinterest with ideas for what to shoot.

This makes the project easier because you have ideas of what to look for. Have a theme for your shots for a week or a month. You can then share with others doing the same project. You can compare your shots to others and see what you can do to improve your shots. Doing it on the website is also a motivator to make you keep taking the shots, every day.

Some other cool things about doing this project. When you look back at the end of the year, you can remember what you did on each day throughout the year. Good or bad because of the instant reminder of that day. I am doing it now. I have a template for Evernote I type ideas for books and topics to write about and a least one picture a day.

My template for Evernote is:

Date June 20, 2017

What I did today

The daily photo

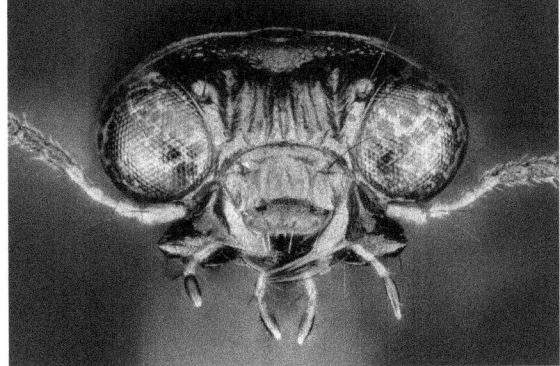

Action items and things to write about
    1.
    2.
    3.

It is a simple easy to use template, I copy the template to the Evernote folder I keep it in and fill it in every day. I sometimes add more photos than one a day, but I always add at least one.

Make sure you always have a camera with you every day. This is much easier now than it was a few years ago. Almost everyone has a phone on them all the time. Most phones now will take shots more than adequate for the project.

Some tips to keep you going through the project.

- Try to tell a story about the day with your shots. Try to use your composition creativity in all your shots and do not snap a shot only to get something to post.
- If you see an excellent shot, take a few minutes to take the shot. Do not think I will get my daily shot later. You may not see another decent shot.
- Keep a notebook or keep notes on your phone. You will have good ideas for a great shot, but you cannot get to it today. They will be useful for future days when you do not know what to shoot.

- If you run out of ideas, set a weekly theme. Such as flowers for this week, or special buildings like barns or churches or skyscrapers.
- Try to post your photos daily or at least once a week so you do not get behind.
- Add notes to your photos, even if only a line, so others will know what is going on and what the story of the photo is.
- Have fun with it and try to stick with it if you can.

Here are some of the places where you can do your project online.

365project.org/

www.blipfoto.com/

www.photoblog.com/

You can also use blogging sites like Blogger.com. Start a blog you can keep your photos on with notes. It is easy to share or keep just for you. you can do the projects on your own website like many people do.

There are other options for where to share your shots. These are some of the most popular ones. Have fun and learn.

If you take on this project, commit to it and stay with it for as long as you can. You will be proud of yourself at the end of the challenge, and you will be a better photographer.

Time Lapse

This project is not one you will learn a lot about photography from the standpoint of taking photos in the normal sense.

What you will learn is a wealth of information about how light varies. When the light for pictures is best, and how things change, sometimes much faster than you thought. You also will learn that the results of the project are impressive.

The traditional way is to take a shot of a spot at intervals of time. This gives you a video by showing the pictures in a sequence. You put them together into a slide show. When shown at a quick speed, you can see what changes over the course of the shooting time. Like a digital version of the flip books that have a different picture on each page.

The main use and what makes time lapse cool is that you can take things that happen over long periods of time and condense it into a couple of minutes or less.

There are several cameras that come with this capability. I have one that will do this. You can set it up on a tripod and set it to take a shot every so often. You can set the time from one second up to 10-hour intervals. It will keep going until the battery dies or the memory card is full.

Another way you can do this project is to take a picture of the same spot at intervals for a set period. For instance, you would take a shot of a garden of beautiful flowers, or even your backyard. You can also take a shot of the same spot over a period. For example. The same location every week over a year and put them together in a slide show. After you reach the end of the year, or whatever time you pick. You run them in a slide show and show how the view changed over the time.

There is also a time-lapse option on the new iPhone that will compress time and speed it up. It is kind of cool, worth checking out. The number of frames per second will be set by the phone, it will take depending on how long you let it go. The longer the time you record the shots, the fewer shots per second it will take. **Here is a great article that explains how it works.** Check it out.

You can also do the project with people. You can take a portrait shot of a person every week. Or once a month, or once a year, for as long as you want, then put them together and show the way they have changed.

Another example of a common use is a series of pictures of a woman going through a pregnancy. You can see the changes over time from the beginning until the end of the pregnancy.

Once you get the pictures taken. There are several software programs you can use to put the slide show together. My favorite program is Proshow Producer, but there are many options.

The concept of time-lapse photography is easy to understand. The actual finished product can be a long time-consuming process if you put together hundreds or thousands of shots in a slide show.

I recommend that you start out with something simple. Try shots of a flower opening, set your camera to take a shot every 30 seconds for a couple of hours and see how it looks.

Depending on the flower you can vary the time between photos to get a nice smooth transition. You can make it look like you made a video of a flower opening, in a matter of a couple of minutes.

Here is an example of a time-lapse. This is of the new world trade center construction. It is hundreds of thousands of pictures taken over nine years. This is an amazing commitment by the photographer, to get this project done.
https://www.youtube.com/watch?v=Nn11DWH_LEA

This is my favorite one. It shows what you can do on bright days with lots of clouds moving across the sky. In several beautiful locations. A great video and a lot of time spent taking the shots.
https://www.youtube.com/watch?v=8gD_9WPPFb4

Here is another link to a whole section of time-lapse videos on YouTube. You can see how cool these are and kill a bunch of time if you want to watch.
https://www.youtube.com/results?search_query=time+lapse&page=2

There is no end to what you can do with time-lapse photography. things you can only show with time-lapse photography.

Shapes

Shapes are one of the best projects you can work on because you can turn this into many projects. There are many shapes you can look for in natural and man-made things.

The way to do this project is to pick a shape. Go out with your camera and look for shapes. All the photos you take must have the shape you pick as the focus point of the photo.

For example. If you pick triangles as your shape, all shots you take on that outing must have the triangle as a main part of the shot.

The great thing about this project is it makes you think, and it forces you to look for and see things you have never seen before.

It will amaze you at the shapes you see when you are looking for them. Shapes you have never seen before and in places you never noticed before.

Two shapes in one shot, a great circle shape with a cross through the center.

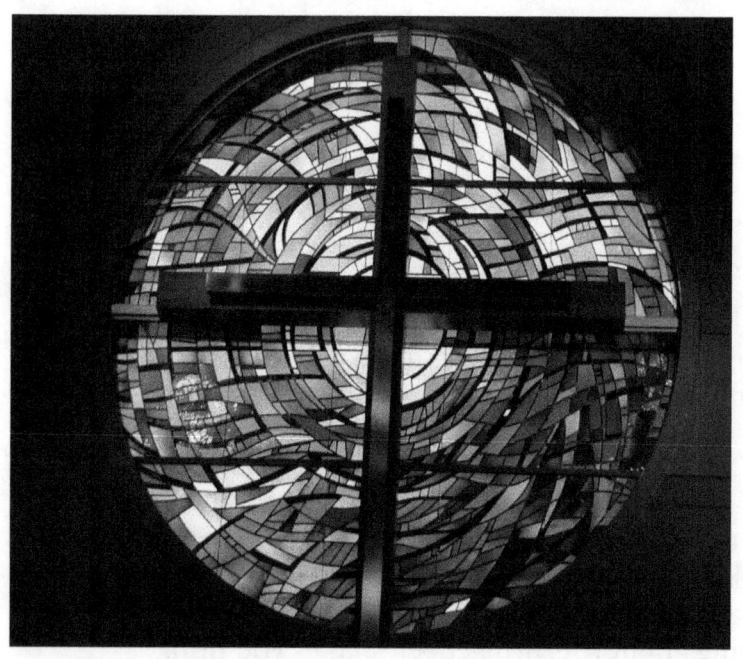

Here is another shot with two shapes in it. The key to shape pictures is to get you to see things you would not see unless you look for them. You look at the object, and you see more shapes. When you look and point them out, it is obvious that they are there.

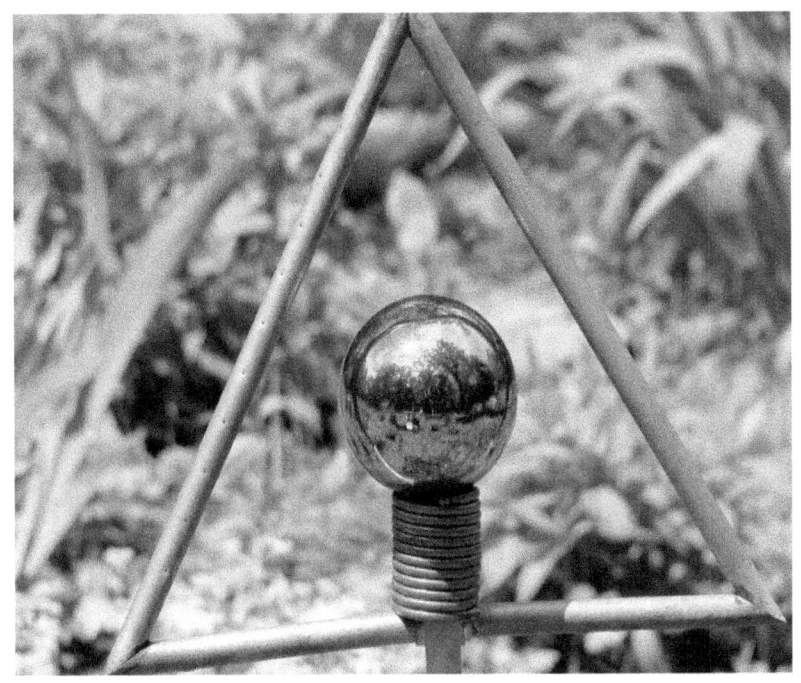

This shot is a good shot of a spherical shape and a triangle. Things like this that you see every day, and you do not even think about the shapes. It is all about looking at everything and seeing everything about it.

The next shot is round or spherical. The vibrant colors make the shot stand out and make it more interesting.

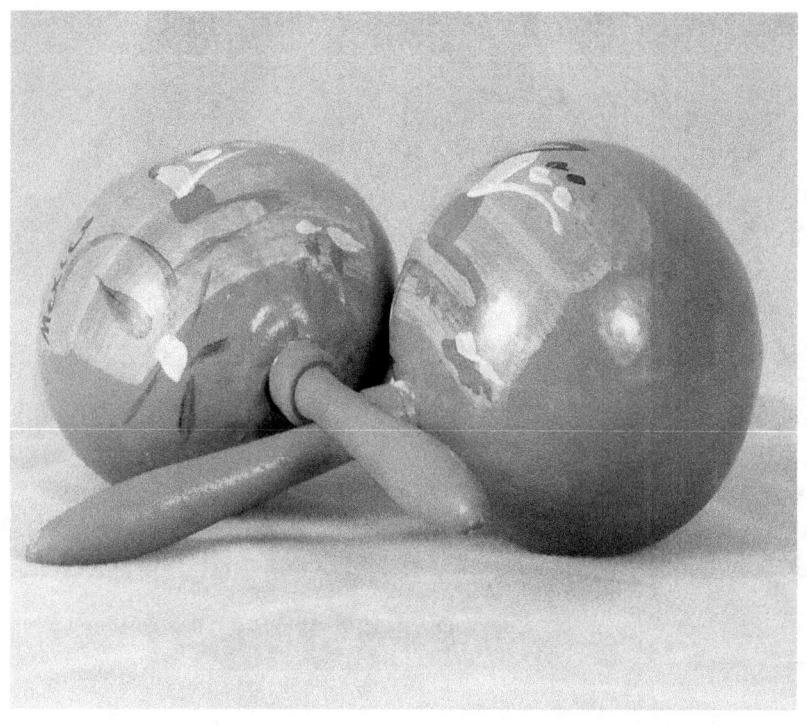

You can pick any shape you want, circles, hearts, rectangles, squares, etc.

This project will get you looking at everything closer. Looking for the shapes in the scene you are looking at. This is a great project to improve your photography. This project is not as much to make great photos, it is more to get you to see things that you miss when not looking for them. It is training your mind to find shapes and see different objects.

Getting the perfect composition. The exact lighting, and the true color and tone. These things are all important.

And you will see these things better because you are looking more at the scenes you see.

This is a great rectangle shot I took in the fall near the Kettle River near Hinckley MN. It is an old logging building that is going back to nature.

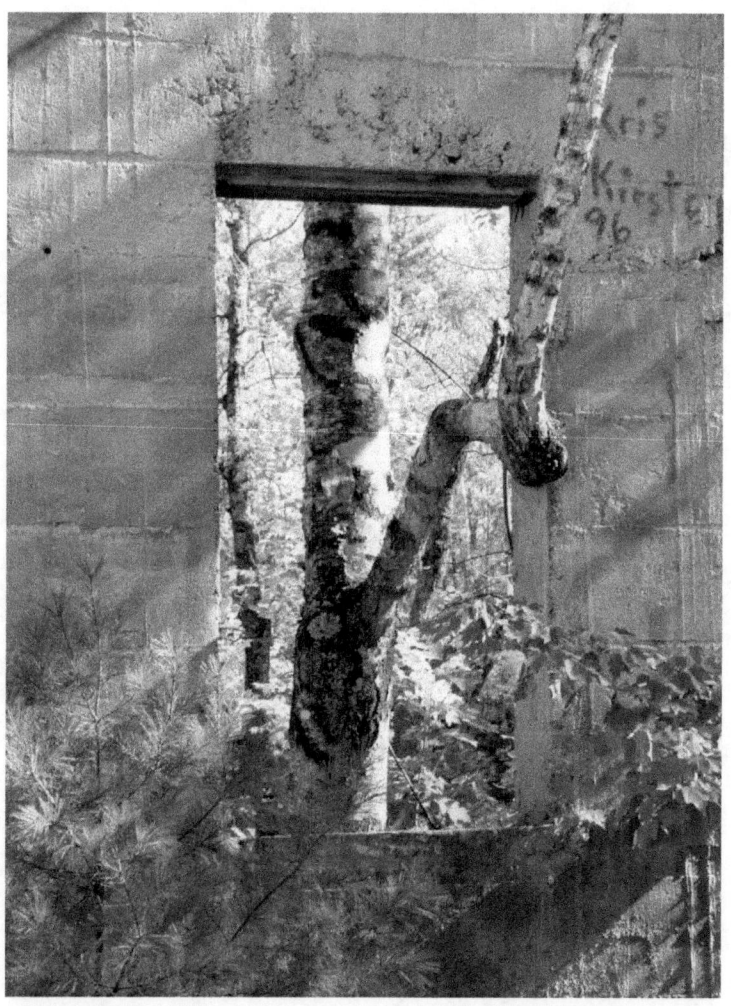

The whole point of this project is to get you to look and see things you would not see most of the time. The benefit to seeing more is that you will use the shapes. You will use them to frame, or focus on the subject better, or make more interesting photos. Again, have fun while you are learning, and you will become a better photographer while you learn.

Pick a shape for a day to shoot, or even for a week. Every shot you look at, look at the shapes and set up the shot.

Aged Things

Aging is a fun project. The point is to go out shooting. Look for things that are dead, or rotting, wearing away, old, etc. Look for anything that has gone past its best times, past its usable time.

It does not mean that something is bad because it is decaying or past its prime. Old people have wrinkled skin and look weathered. These portraits can be fantastic.

Some of the most memorable portraits from Time magazine or National Geographic are portraits of older people that use texture to show age. Here is a great age and texture shot that is enhanced by the wrinkles. The texture pops out of the photo.

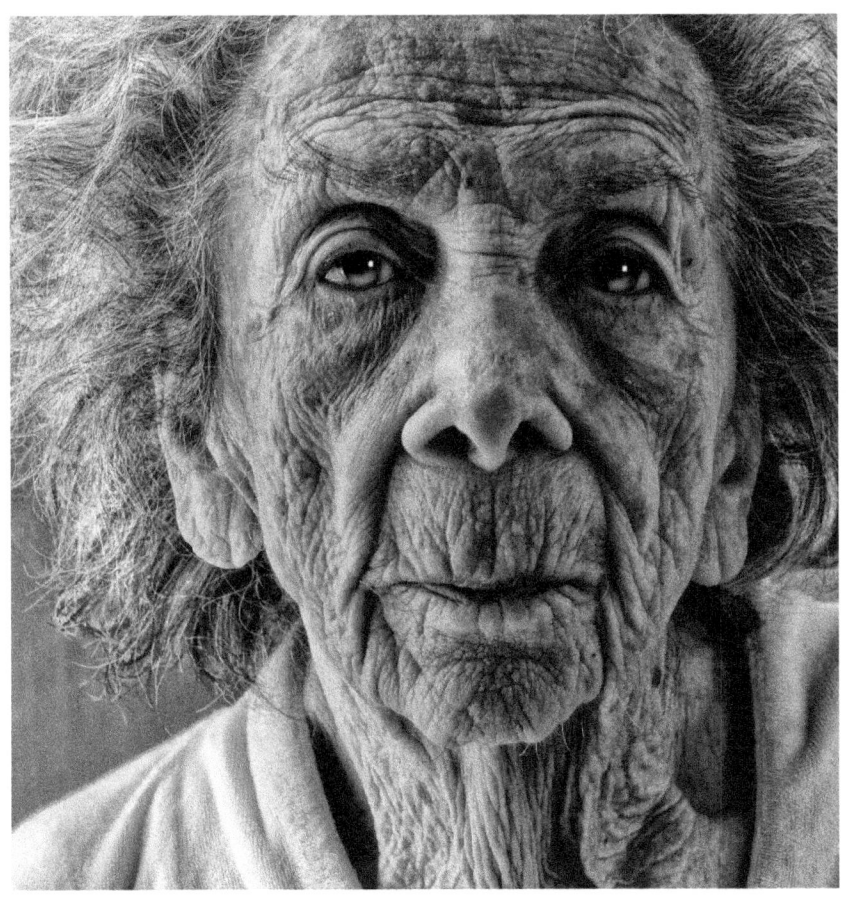

Things you can use to show aging.

- Old people
- Rotting plants
- Rotting teeth
- Abandoned buildings.
- Broken-down buildings
- Old cars

- Old rotting anything

Anything you find that shows something past its prime.

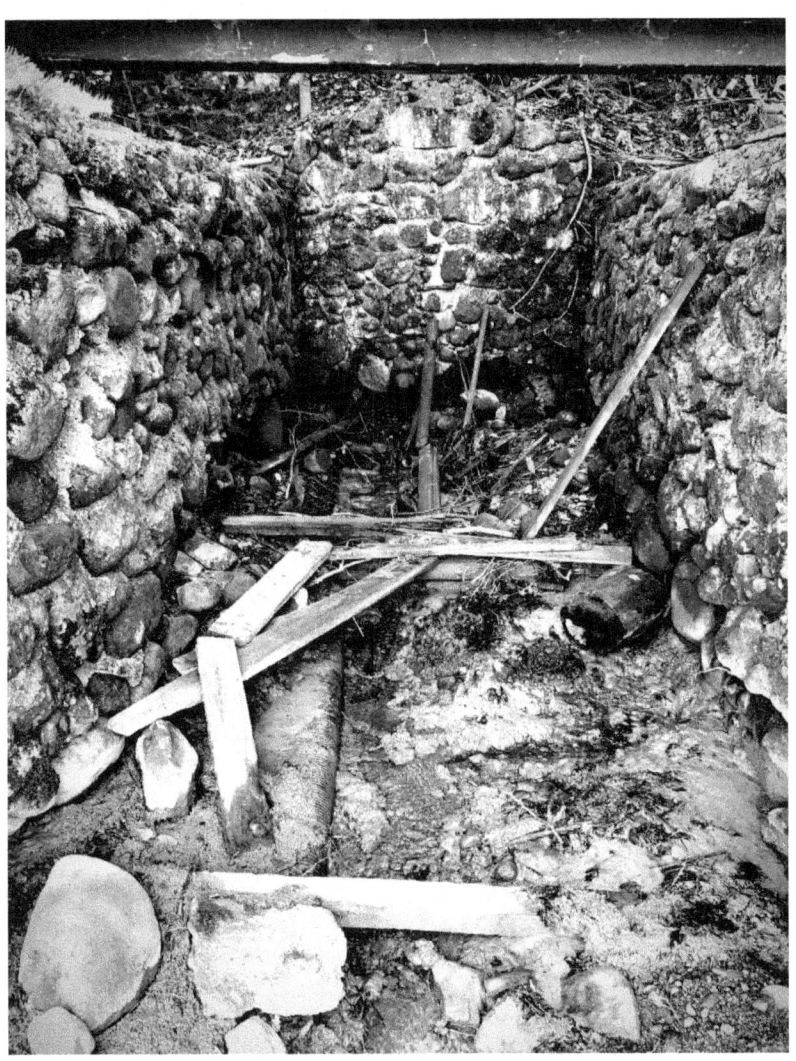

This is a great shot of the old falling down boat house at
my in-law's cabin in central Minnesota.

The boathouse was solid and well built, but it is past its time. It is all rocks from the lake mortared together. There is a spring that comes out of the hill in the back, and the water has been eating away at it for many years.

Some things get better as they age. If you watch the TV show American Pickers, they think everything gets better with age. Some of the old things they pick look like trash. However, they sell them for a lot of money because they are old and rare.

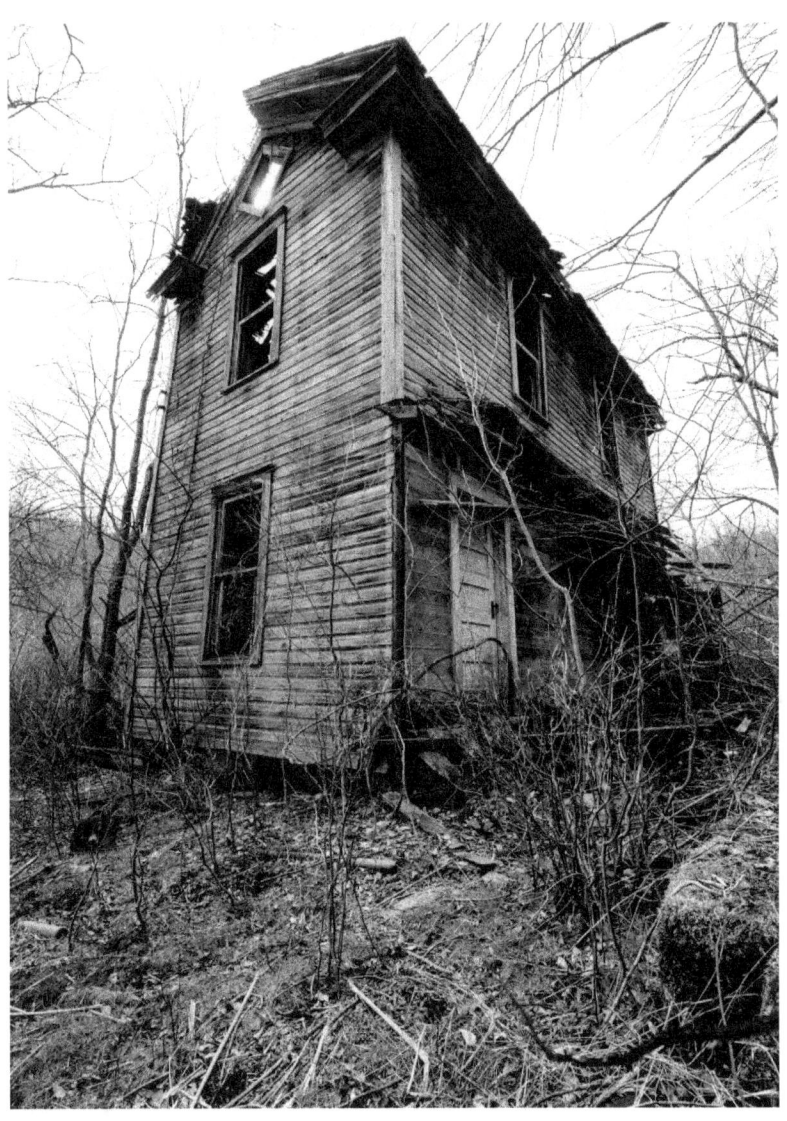
Here is a wonderful decaying house that makes a great shot.

I love old wood barns; they are one of my favorite things to take pictures of. I am sure that in another 25 years, there will not be any wooden barns left.

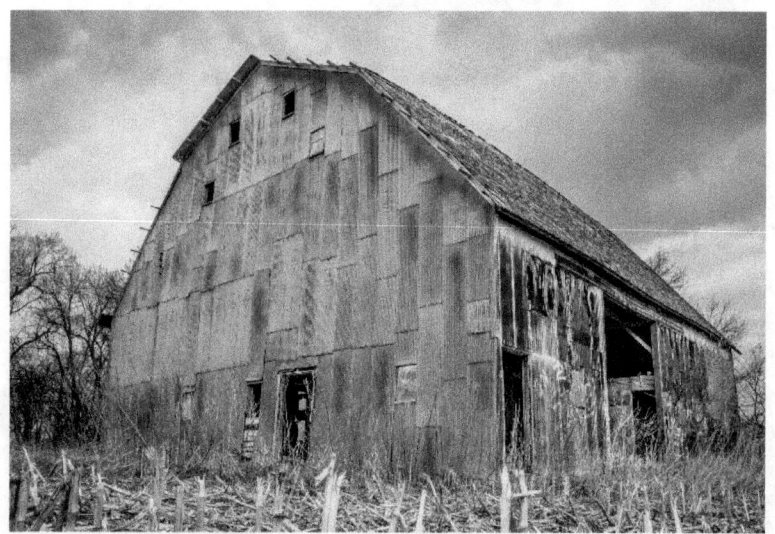

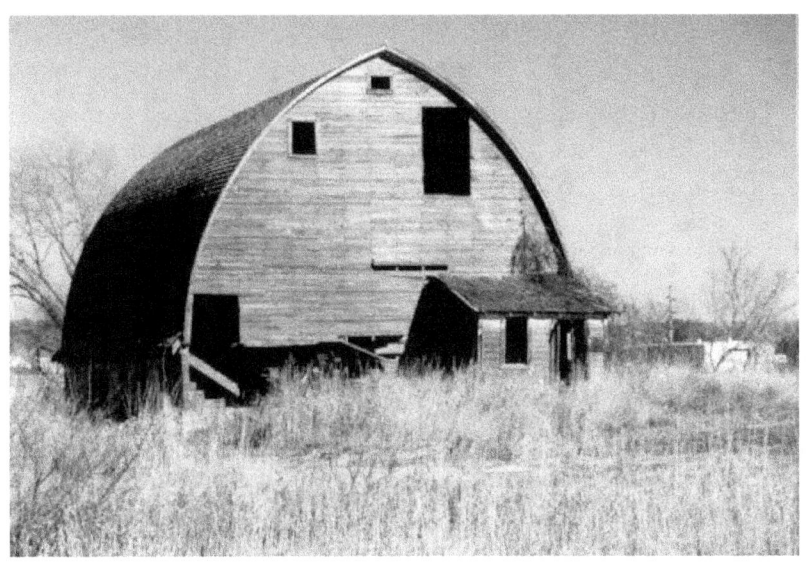

Like I said, old barns are one of my favorite things to shoot. I have hundreds of shots of wood barns. My perfect job would be to get a motor home and with my wife, drive around the country taking shots of old barns and old churches, which is another of my favorite things to shoot.

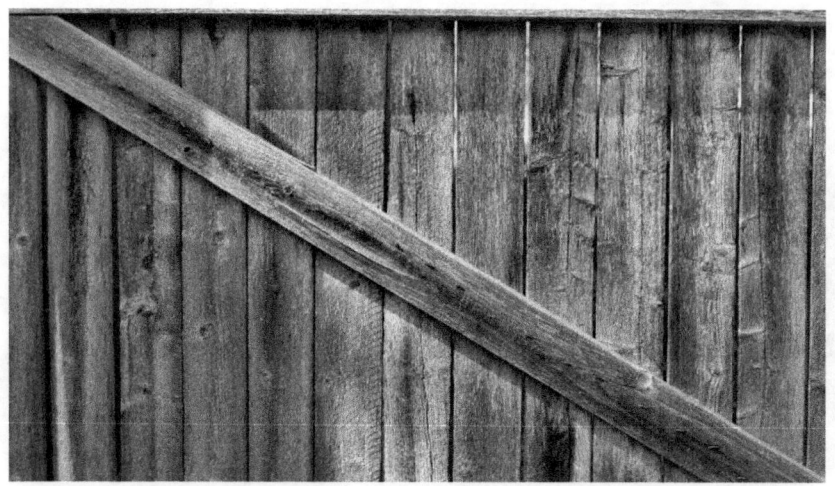

This is an aged cedar fence in the backyard at my former
house. Decay looks cool and can make an interesting
photo. Some things like Cedar have a more pleasant look,
and most people like it better as its ages.

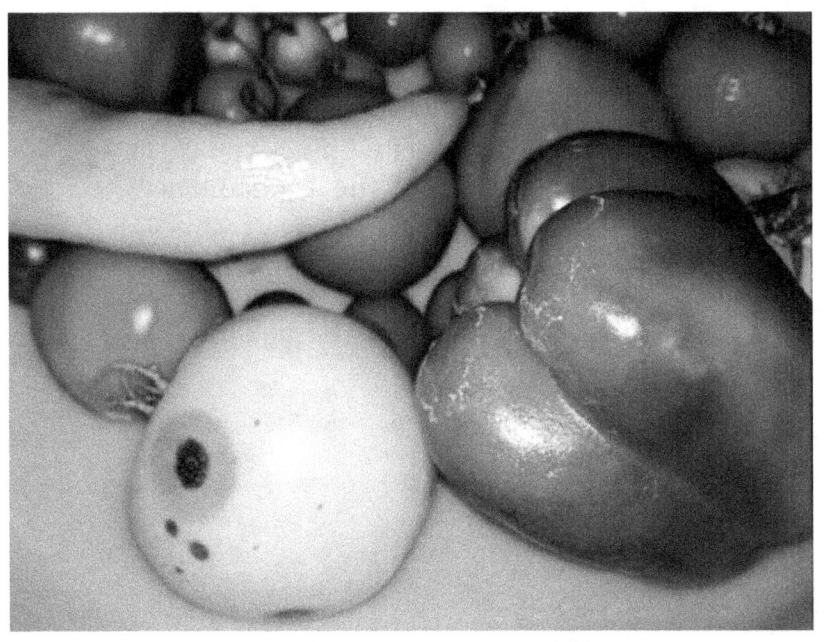

Some rotting veggies still have good color but
deteriorating.

Textures

Texture is a fun project. There are so many things you can find that have texture. The shot above of the wooden fence gate is an excellent texture and aging shot. You can find great texture shots almost everywhere you look. Look around your house, look at the ceiling, walls, carpet flooring, etc. Look in your yard or in your car. Look for texture everywhere you look.

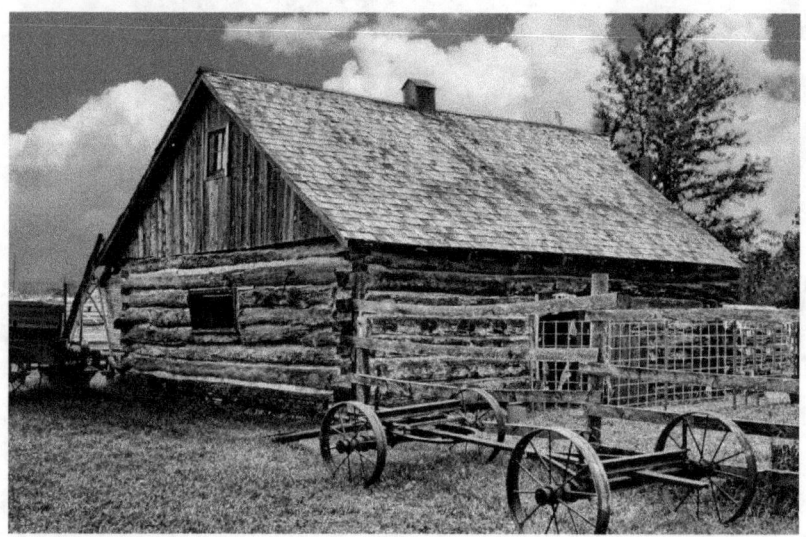

This is a favorite shot of mine. There is texture in the barn, the fence, and the grass. The point of this project is to force yourself to look closer at everything you are shooting. Look at how texture makes your shot more interesting. If you picture the above shot with smooth siding on the cabin, no grass on the ground, and a smooth metal roof, the shot would be much less appealing.

The next shot is a great texture shot that shows what hoar frost is. And what it does when it forms on trees and grass and everything it touches. It is something that many people living in warmer climates will never see. Even in northern climate we only see it once a year on average. If you can get out and shoot it when it happens, you can get fantastic shots many people will never see.

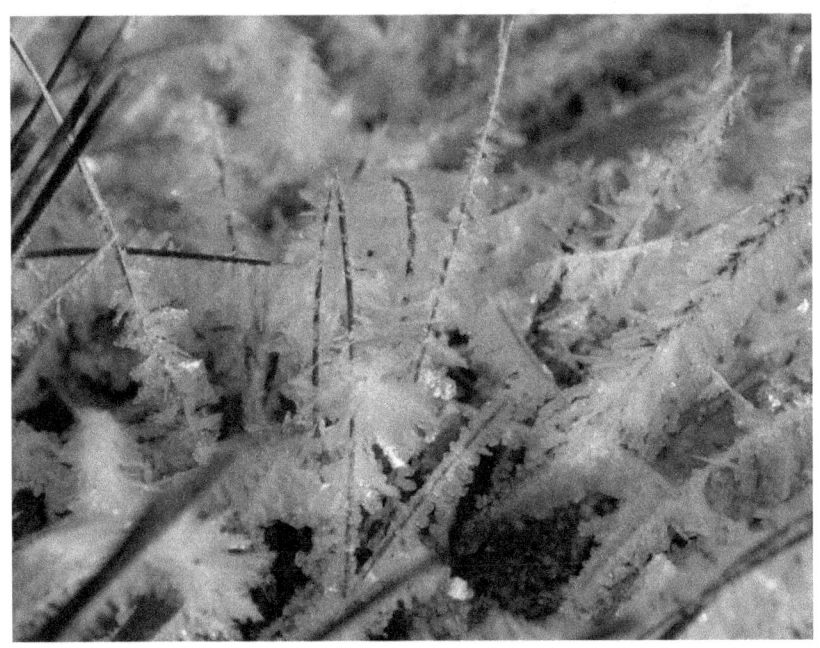

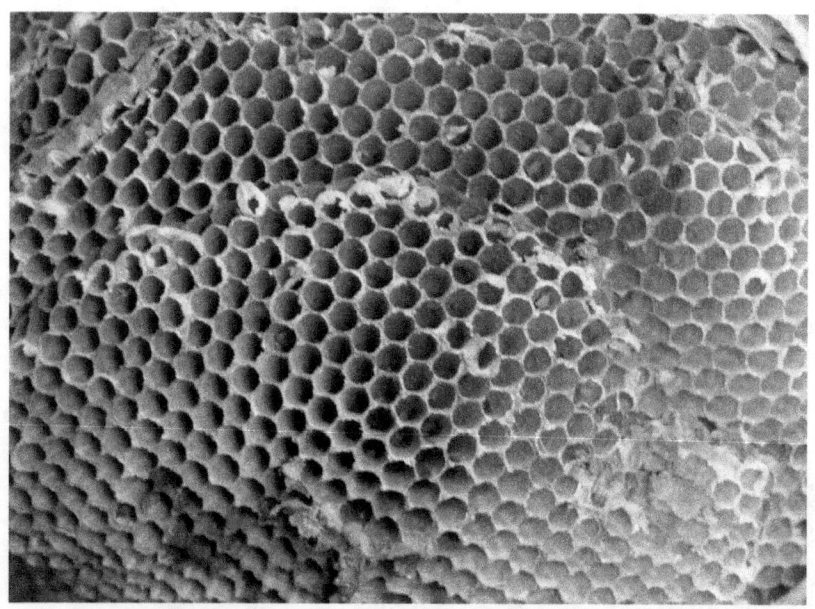

The shot above is a shot of a large wasp nest. A nest that was in a tree in our yard. It shows great texture, and the amazing way wasps create a cool nest.

Look at everything around you when you are walking through your yard and everywhere else. Look at everything from a photographer's perspective. You will see things no one else notices, and that you have never noticed before.

Seeing things that other do not, will make you a better photographer all by itself. Harsh side lighting is something you can use in texture shots. It brings out the texture more than flat strait on lighting.

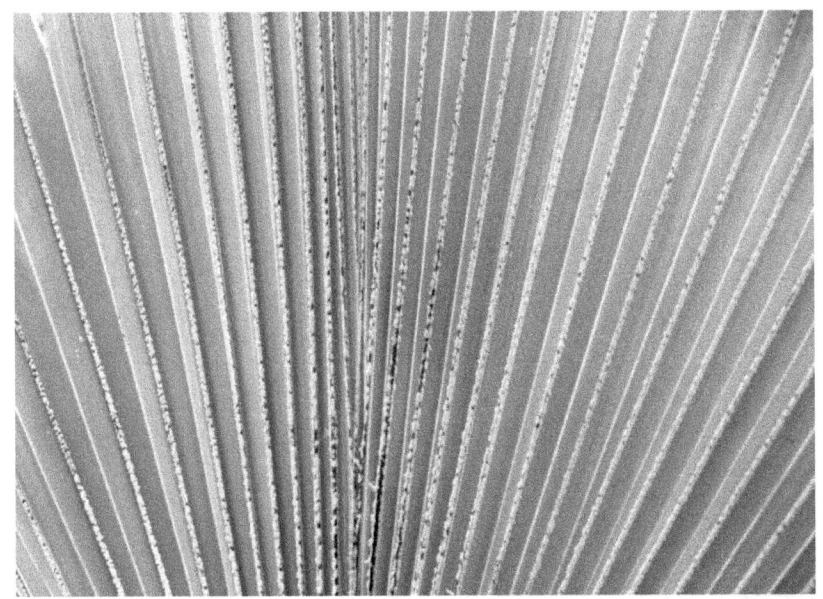

This shot is of a huge palm leaf at a Como park in Minnesota. There is texture in the folds of the leaf and the little white bumps on the edge of the fold.

Como Park in St Paul Minnesota is one of my favorite places to go hunting for great photos. I have been going there to take pictures for over 30 years. I have taken close to 10,000 shots there, photos of many subjects.

The park has an outstanding zoo. With a fantastic indoor tropical garden. It also has an outdoor Japanese garden, a beautiful golf course and a several hundred-acre park. It is a popular park on nice summer days. It can be terribly busy, so you need to go there during the week, or early morning on weekends to get the good photos. Or to even find a place to park.

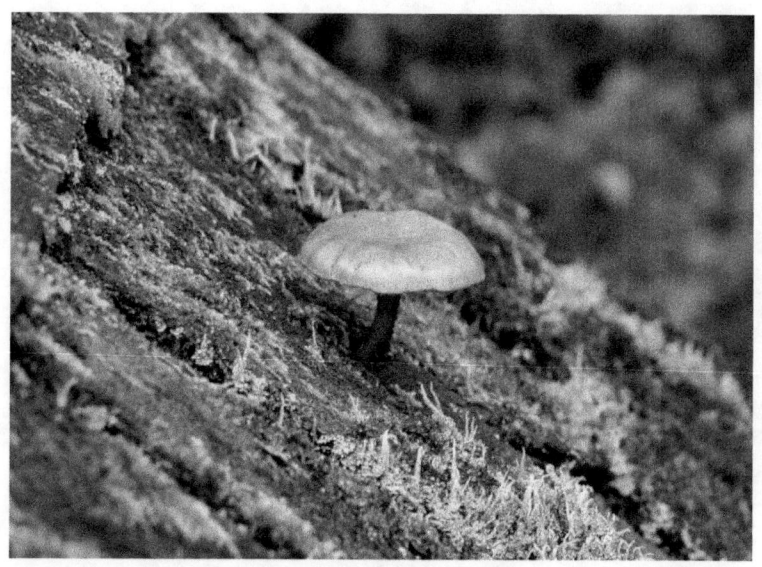

This shot is another one I made in my yard. The wishing well in chapter 3 was in a shady spot in the yard. It grew moss on it most of the time but this year the moss was much bigger, and a bonus was the mushroom.

This shot is a perfect example of what texture adds to a photo. The mushroom is a cool item by itself, but the texture of the moss and the decaying wood adds a lot to the shot.

In your yard

The project is all about in your yard. Go into your yard and look at everything, look at things in a different way than normal. Look at everything.

Try to create a good shot from normal objects in your yard. If you do not have a yard, go to a local park. Look at things from a photography point of view. Get down low and look at things from ground level.

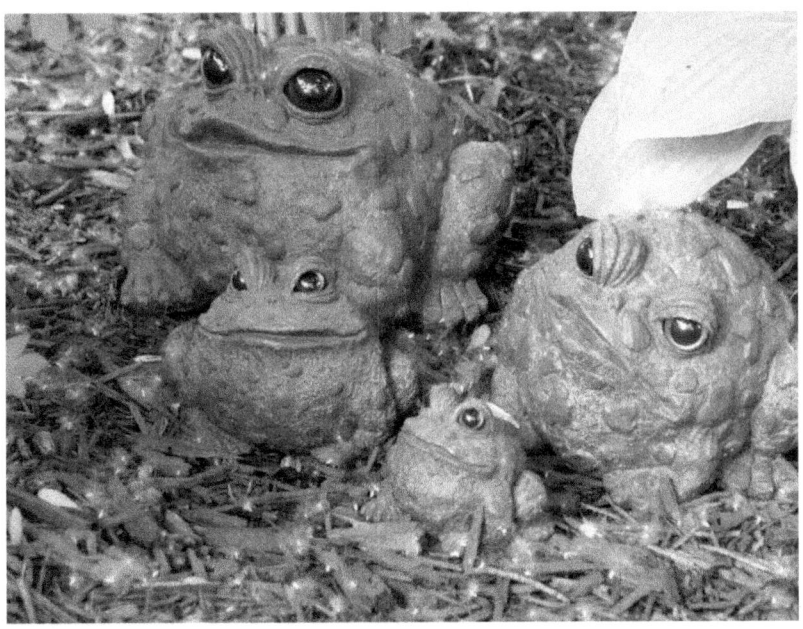

My wife has frogs in the garden. Adding in the plants and the cottonwood seeds. This adds more interesting objects in the shot without taking away from the point of the shot, which are the frogs. The shot below is a cool stature that my wife got somewhere. I added the flowers to the shot to bring in more color while the girl statue is the main subject.

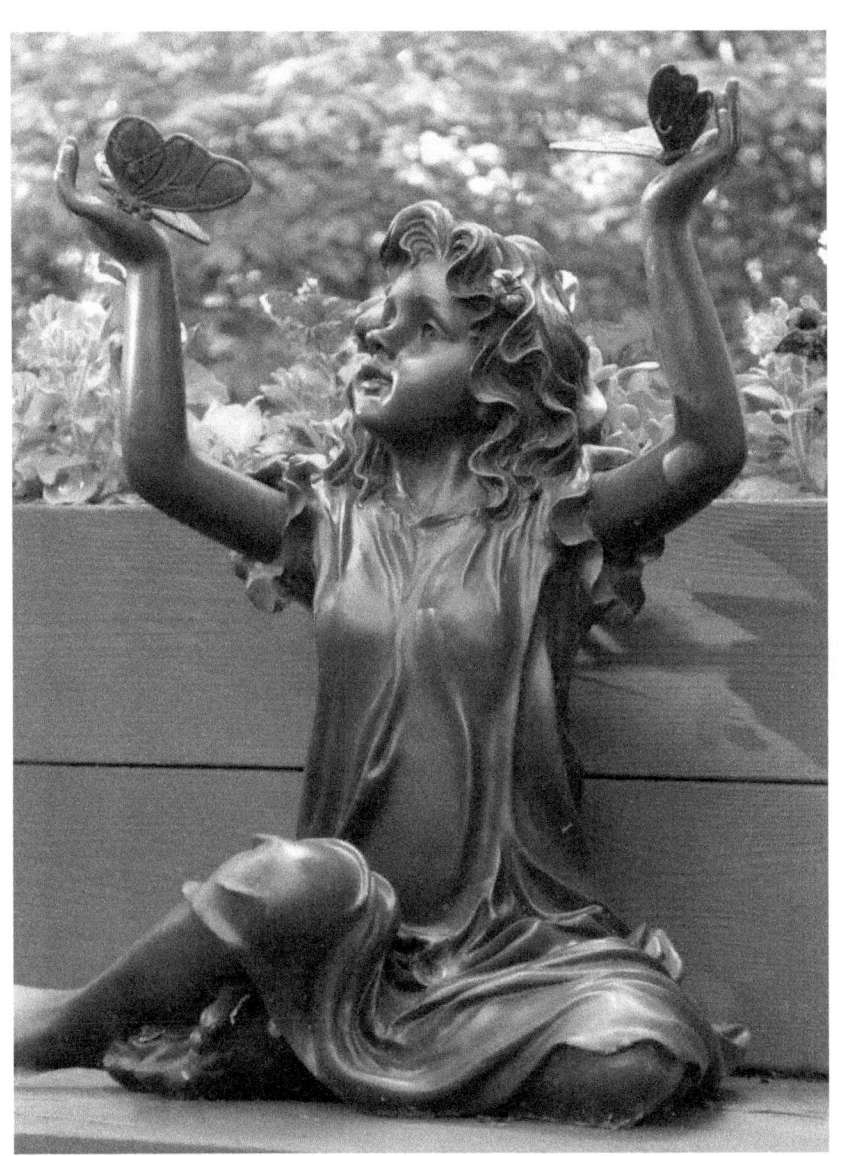

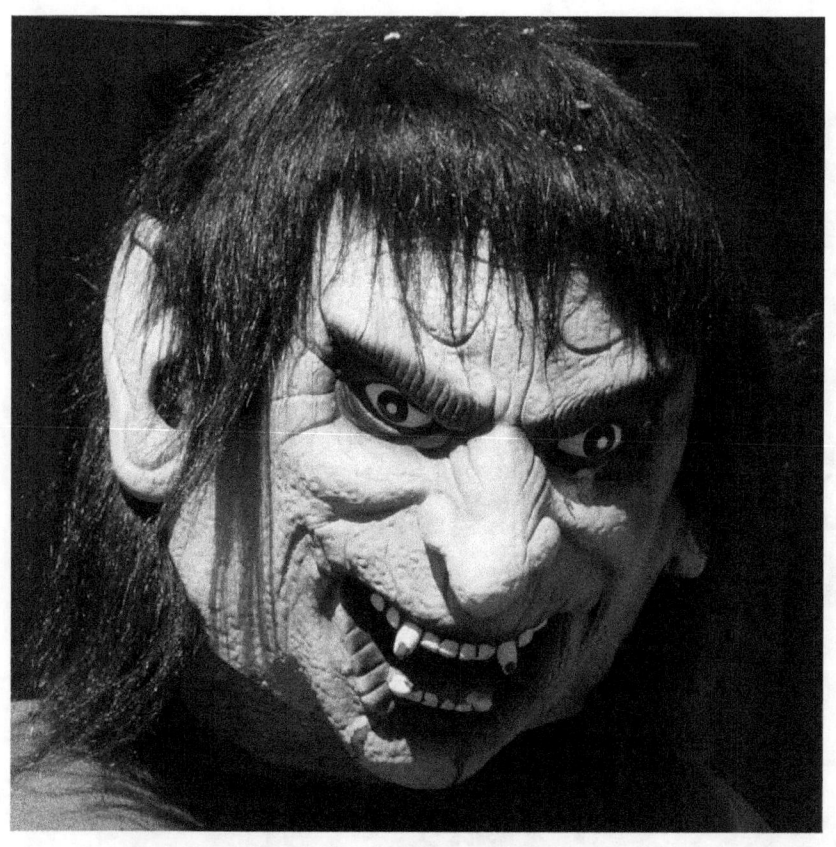

This is a shot of a Halloween decoration. It was a full body size creature. My wife bought it from a guy who had a bunch of Halloween decorations for sale on the side of the road. It was in Anoka Minnesota, the Halloween capital of the world. There were many pieces we had for several years; they were a scary hit for the kid who came to the door trick or treating.

Below is a chipmunk that came up to eat a piece of bread while I was sitting on the deck. We had many families of chipmunks living in our yard; they were fun to watch. I had a couple of them run across my foot one day while they were chasing each other.

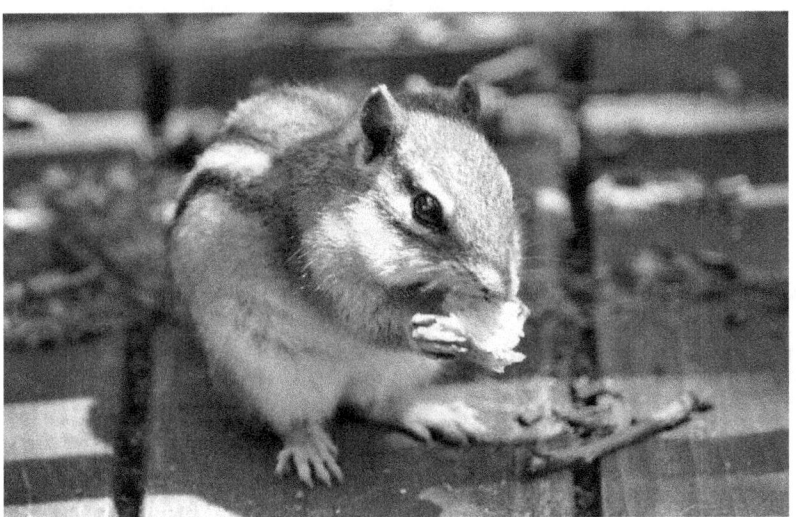

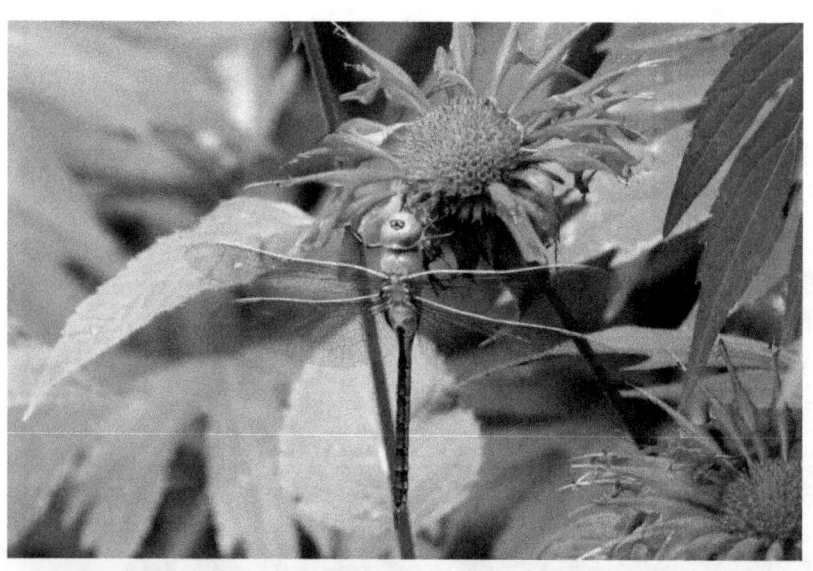

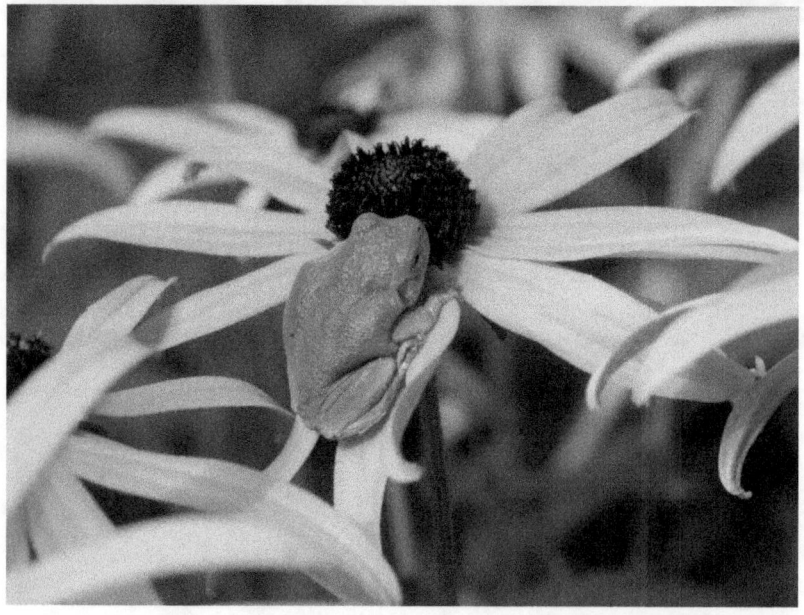

The shots above were in our garden. My wife had a great garden in our yard. The flowers looked awesome, but the dragonfly in the top one and the frog in the lower were posing for the shots. I have over 10,000 pictures I took in our yard over 10 years. If I were not looking, I would not have even seen these animals.

Many of them became cool memories of the different things in our yard. Creatures that were coming and going and living in the yard. Most of these things I would never have seen if I would not have gone looking for them. Many of the shots I took of flowers in the garden, showed up things I did not see when I took the shots. Bugs and other interesting creatures.

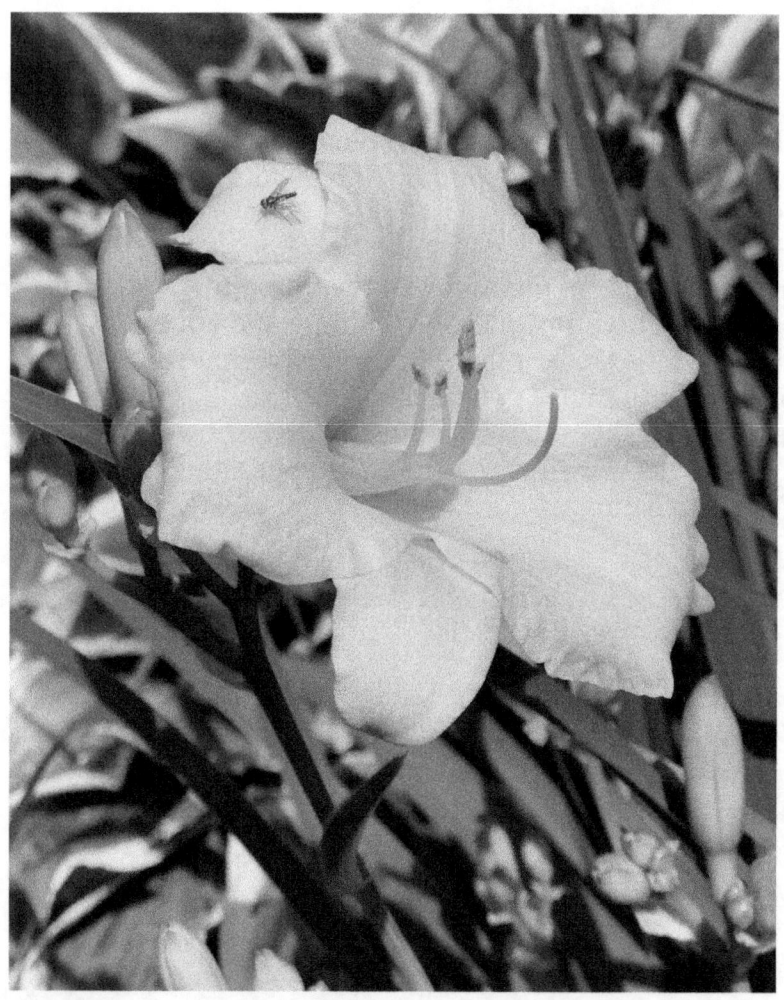

When I looked at them on the computer, there was
something cool in the shot that was a bonus. Some cool
looking bugs or other creatures. Things I found looking for
things to shoot, and there they were. I would never have

seen this bug if I had not been out in the yard looking for photos with camera in hand.

All in focus

To get the whole shot in focus, you need to understand at least the concept of hyper focal distance. Hyperfocal distance is the closest distance you can focus in front of you. And still have the shot in focus all the way to infinity.

You can calculate hyperfocal distance. To calculate it is rather complex. There are tips you can use to get a good enough guess so you can get good sharp shots. Learning the calculations will give you the ability to estimate and make it work. Once you know about where to focus, it will help you get the shot in focus from front to back.

The best setup is to use a wide-angle lens with the smallest aperture you can. The distance will change and get farther away as you zoom out and as you use a bigger aperture. One of the great advantages of digital photography is you can look at the shot and zoom in and make sure the foreground items are sharp. You can shoot it again if not.

One of the fantastic things about phone cameras now is they are great at setting the shot to give you great depth of field. If you want to get serious and know the exact point. You can calculate the point, then use a laser measuring device to show the exact point to focus. A better and more affordable way is to use a cheat sheet to see what it is, then estimate where to focus. Here is a link to Google search images you can copy and carry it with you on your phone for reference.

 The best landscape shots are in focus front to back. It can be very frustrating when you think you have a great shot, and some things you want in the shot are out of focus.

 Here is a great example of front to back sharp focus.

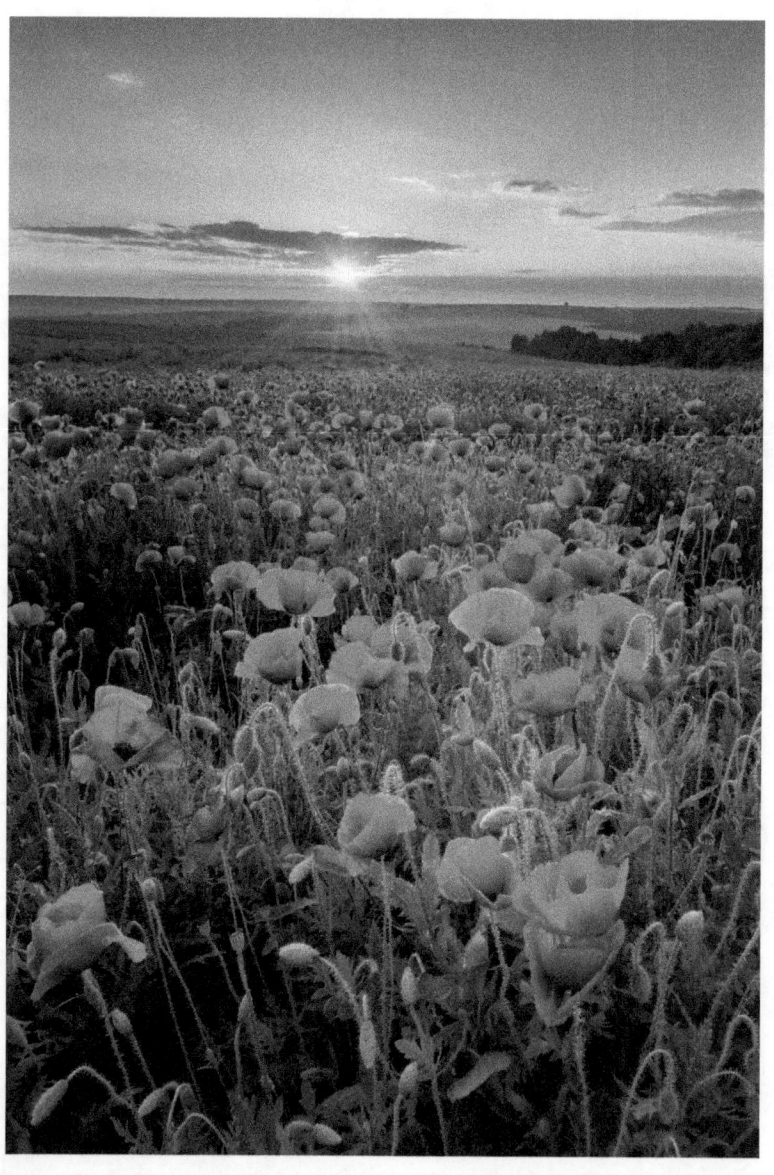

Practice using the hyperfocal distance and focusing where you take the shot from. A general rule of thumb is to focus about one third of the way into the shot. That way you get most of the shot in focus from front to back.

This is one of my favorite shots I have ever taken. You notice the rocks in the foreground are in as sharp a focus as is the rest of the shot. All the way to the lighthouse and the clouds, the whole shot is in focus. To take good landscape shots, you want the whole scene in focus front to back.

If you learn to do this right your landscape shots will be much better and much more enjoyable. If you are off a little, you can crop the shot to make sure the focus stays sharp front to back. The best landscape shots have foreground items in them for scale and interest.

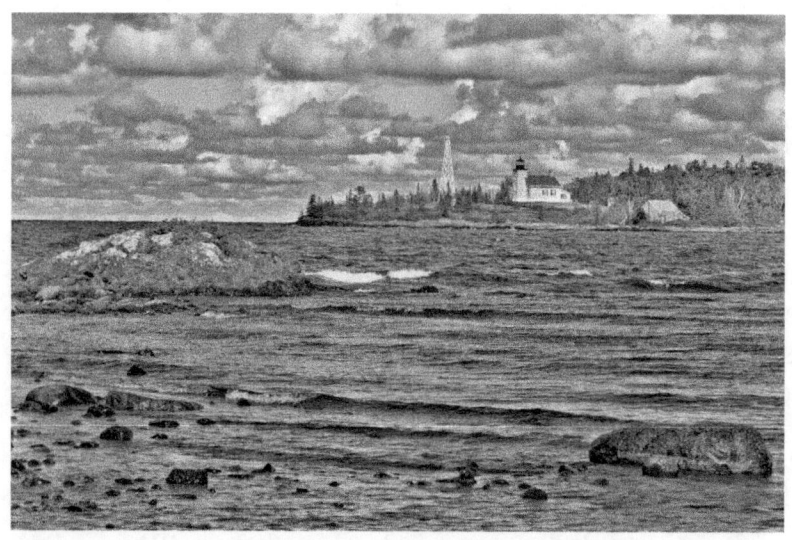

The shot below is another perfect example. See how the rocks and bushes in the foreground all in focus are all the way to the water in the clouds behind. I cannot stress enough how important this is to make good landscape photos.

There are times you want to have parts of the shot blurred. This is, so it focuses the attention about your shot. But most of the time, you want the whole shot in focus, front to back.

Sometimes you will take pictures that have the foreground out of focus. You can fix it sometimes by cropping that part out. But a lot of times the foreground has something in it you want to use for scale for the whole picture. You do not want to crop out.

Try to concentrate on getting the shot in focus front to back when you take it.

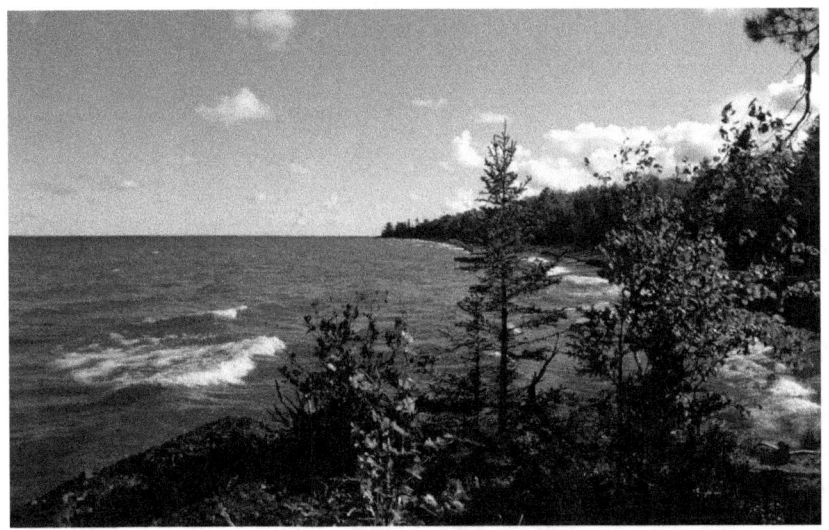

The shot below is different. Even though it is a landscape shot, it is not as far out of a view, but you still want to get it all in focus front back. The flowers in the foreground add a lot to the picture. The statue is the main subject of the picture but without the flowers it is not as nice to look at. Close ups like this are where it is important to use a wide lens. If you zoom in on this with a zoom lens, it will narrow the depth of field and will not be in focus front to back. Zoom by getting closer instead of with the lens.

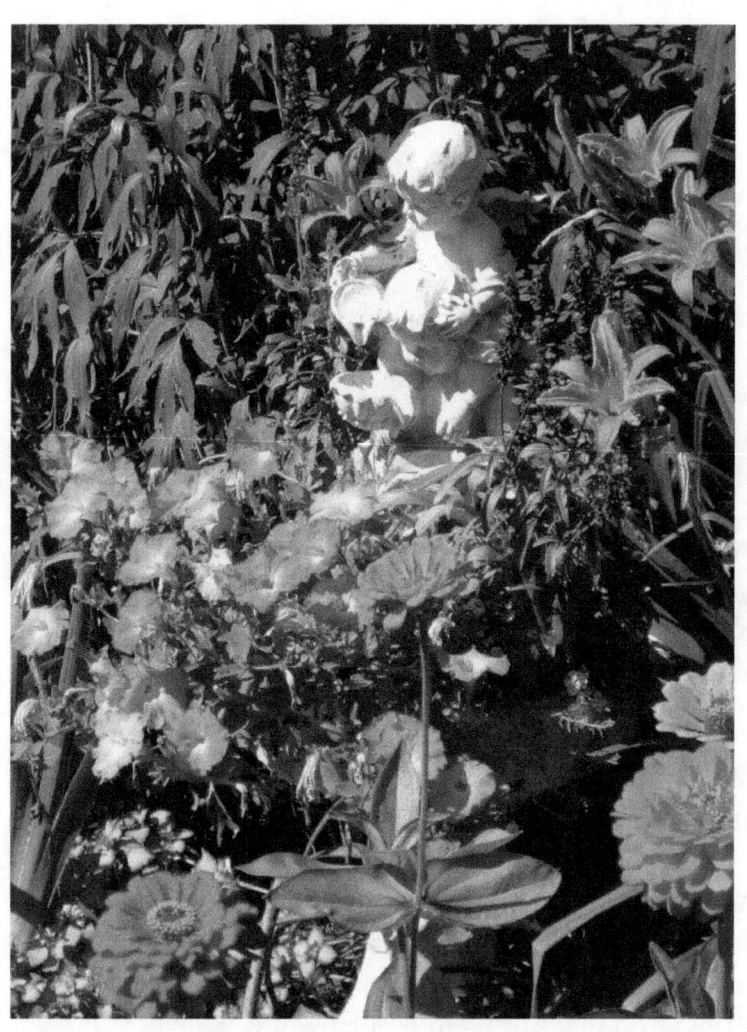

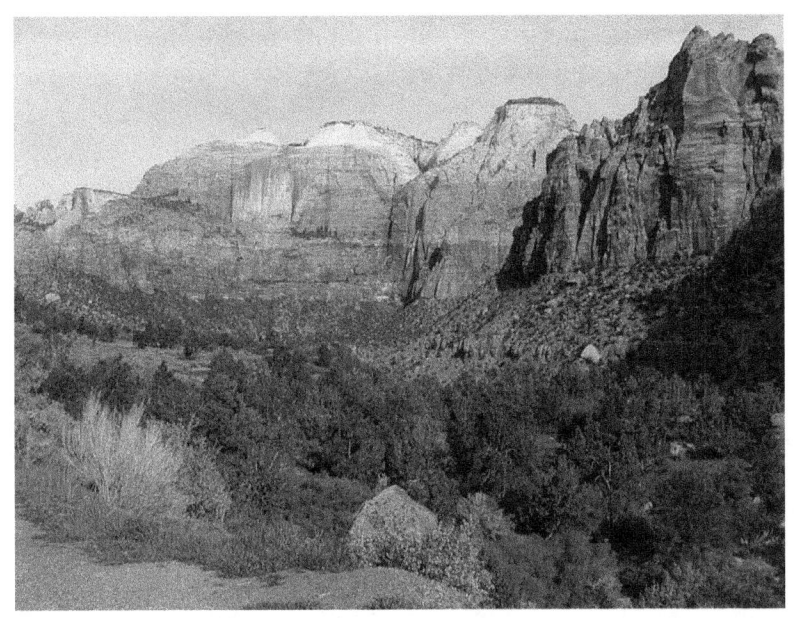

The scene above is from Zion national Park. If you notice the rocks and close foreground are in focus. The shot has the beautiful cliffs and rocks in the background also in focus.

If you look at the picture and imagine foreground being out of focus and blurry. You can see it takes a lot from the shot; it does not make the picture as interesting.

Having the foreground in focus also frames the shot. Framing the shot often adds interesting items to the shot. All these things add to making the shot better.

One thing I always try to do is look at a picture after I take it. Notice where your eyes go. What is the first thing you see when you look at the picture? It should be the cliff in the background the different colors and rocks, their shapes against the sky.

After your eyes focus on the main subject. You look around different parts of the picture. That is when you see foreground subjects. The tumbleweeds, the bushes, everything that adds to this shot.

One more example of full shot focus is another one of my favorite pictures. This picture taken at Bryce Canyon National Park. North of where the needles are. The snowcapped mountain in the background is 87 miles from this point. It is an amazing view on this clear day.

There are so many interesting things in the shot. The trees in the foreground add to it. As does the colored rocks in the middle. Then the snowcapped peaks in the back to bring the whole shot together.

The framed shot in Chapter twenty-three is from the same spot. I zoomed in and used the trees to frame the mountains in the shot. It is a great example of how you can get a different look and perspective without even moving.

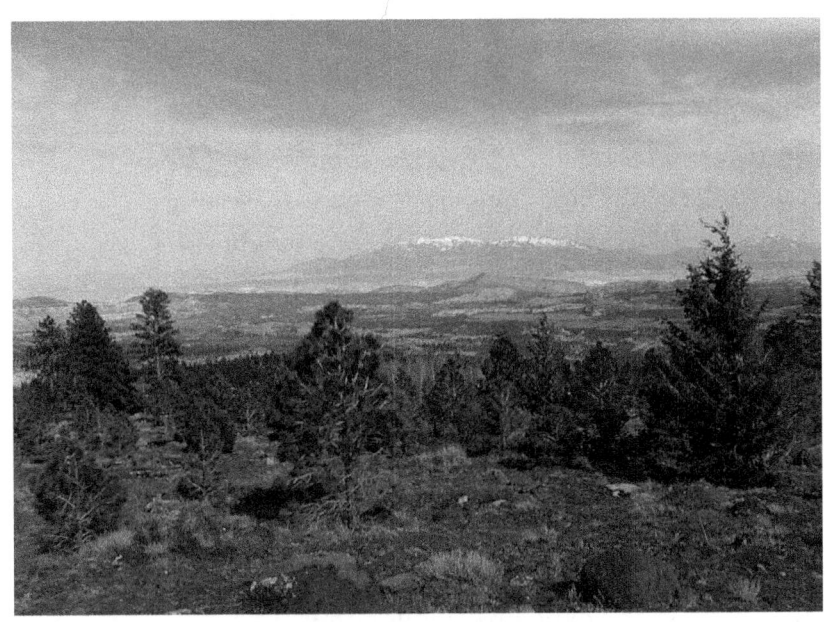

I cannot stress enough how important it is for good landscape shots to have a shot in focus front to back. The way to do that is to check the hyperfocal distance. Then get out there and practice. That is how you figure out where you must shoot to get the best focus front back.

Sunsets

One key to getting the best sunset shots is to have shot in focus front to back. While making sure the exposure is right. Play with the ISO settings on camera. Also, where you take the meter reading, make sure you get the right exposure. Metering higher or lower in the shot can make a huge difference in how the shot looks. Look at the options, but do not take too long. You have a small window of time to get the best sunset shots.

Knowing where the sun should be in the picture is sometimes difficult. Because you are pointing the lens at the sun makes getting the exposure challenging. Try metering above the sun, with it out of the shot, then try below, with the sun out of the shot. You will see a big difference. Once you get the metering you like, lock the metering by holding the button part way, then compose the shot and take it. On your phone you can touch the screen and move the metering point to where it gives you the look you want. One huge advantage of digital cameras is you can see results right away.

The picture below is one of my favorite sunset pictures of all time. The whole picture, front to back is in focus. Showing the interesting foreground items. The waves, and the interesting background items with the sun right on the horizon. The best sunset shots also have good clouds in them. The colors are perfect in this shot. Everything worked perfect for this shot. I locked the metering for the shot to the right of the sun, so the sun was out of the meter point. Using spot metering on your camera can also help get the best lighting in these shots.

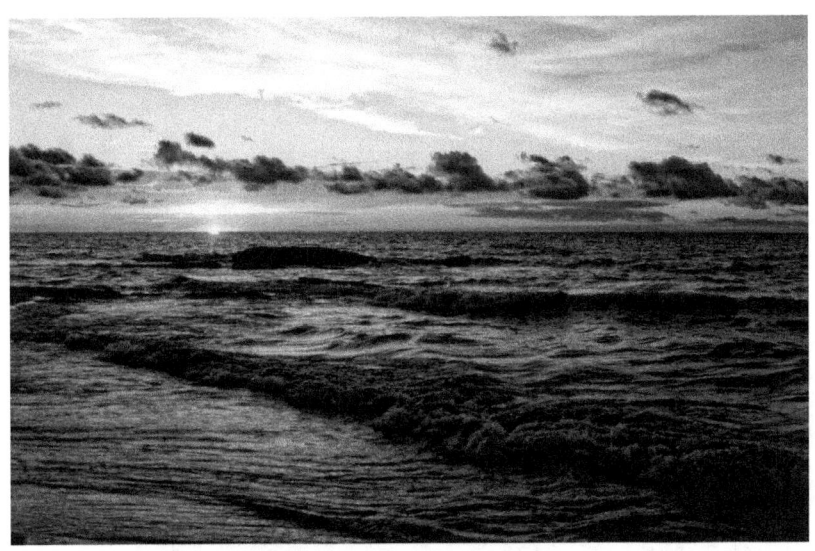

One of the bad things about taking sunset shots is that you only have 5 to 10 min. of perfect light to get the shot you want.

When you get the opportunity for a good sunset picture be ready take a lot of shots. Conditions will change by the minute. What you see in this picture above, will be different in a minute or two.

If you want to get the best pictures of sunsets you want to be there at least 20 min. ahead of time so you can prepare and be ready when the light is right.

This shot is one I took at my brother in laws cabin, the shot is from the shore on a beautiful summer night. I picked a couple of things in this picture that made it stand out. I got into a position, so the doc was leading into the sunset. The colors are nice, and the shot turned out like I wanted to.

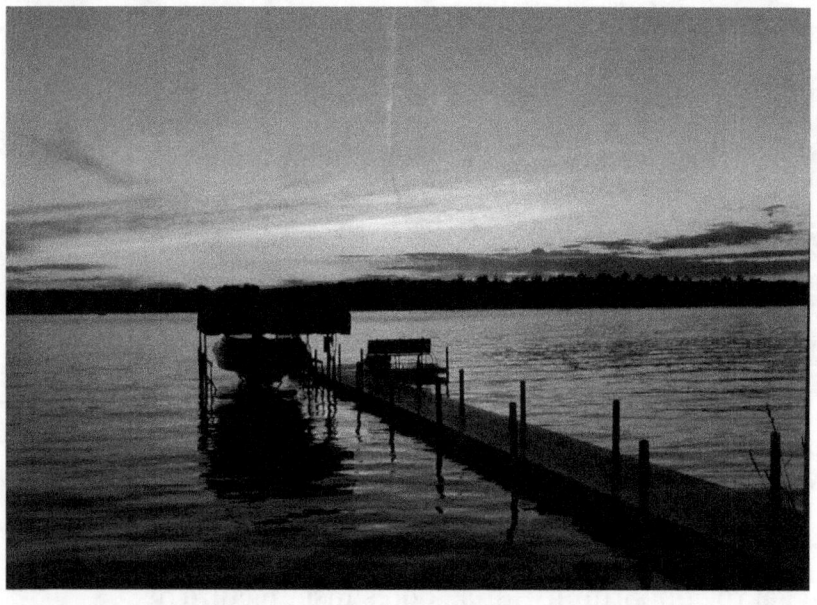

Here is a shot from Florida on the gulf coast I took earlier this year.

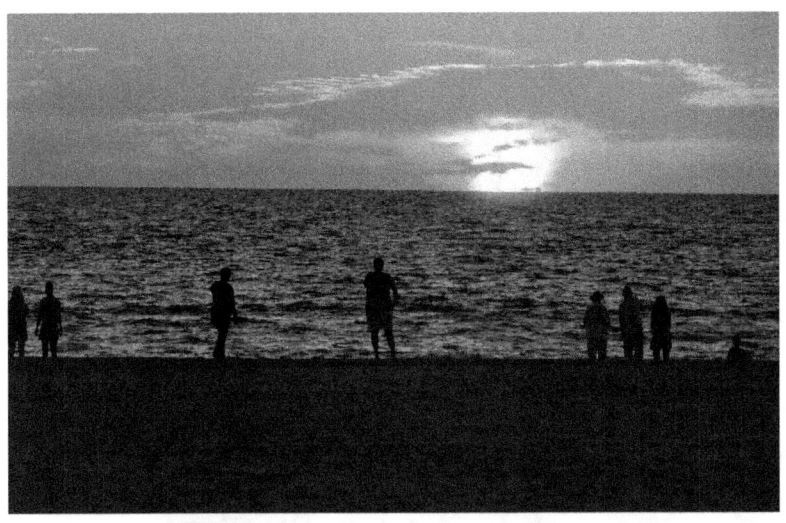

Sunset shots are great to look at. Even if you were not there because they are so relaxing; they give you a calm feeling. Most of the time there is nothing else going on picture that is what makes it so relaxing. Again, you want to focus on getting the shot clear and focused front to back, so the viewer gets the whole experience.

This next picture is one I took a different lake where I was fishing at sunset. The boat was going by at the right time, and I got the shot. The boat added something great to the photo. I had a camera with me, so I am always ready.

Sunset shots are hard to predict before you see what you want to shoot. So, you must be ready to make the picture. One thing nice now is almost everyone has a phone that will take decent pictures. So, if you always have your phone with you, you can at least know you will get the shot. It may not look as good as if you had your digital camera but at least you get it.

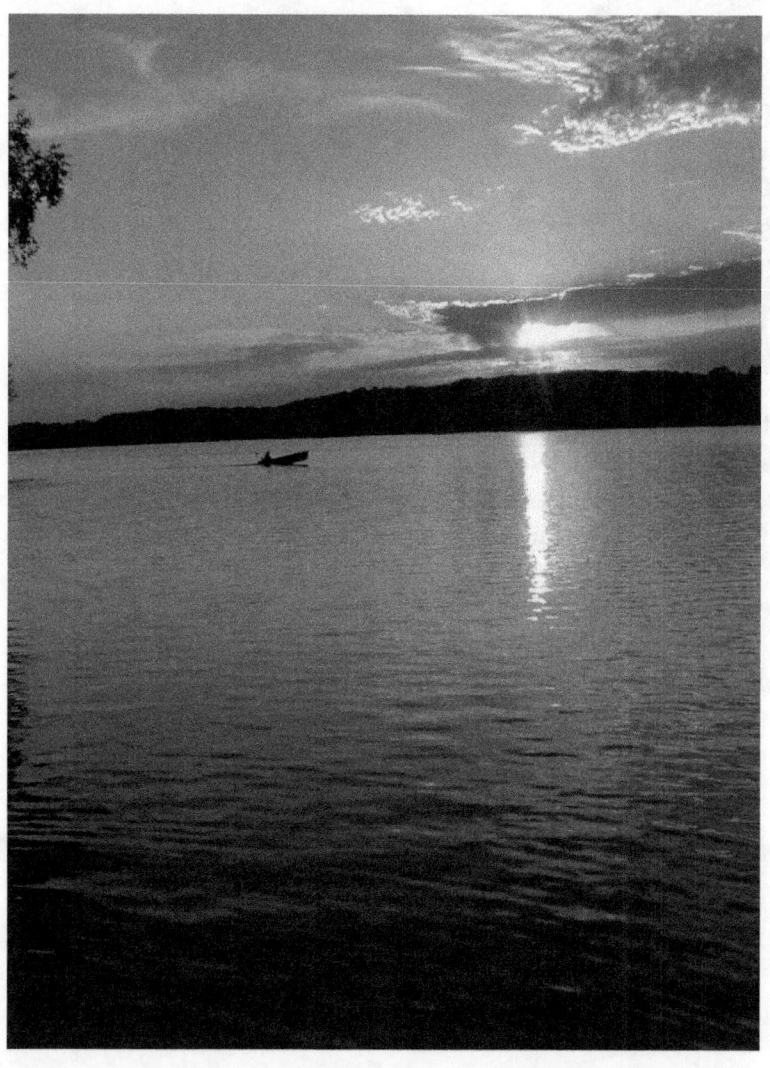

The shot below is what the first shot from above looked like a couple of minutes later.

It is still a good sunset picture, but it is not the same and it is not as dramatic. There are different levels of sunset shots because they change so quick. That is why you need to be there before the best ones happen.

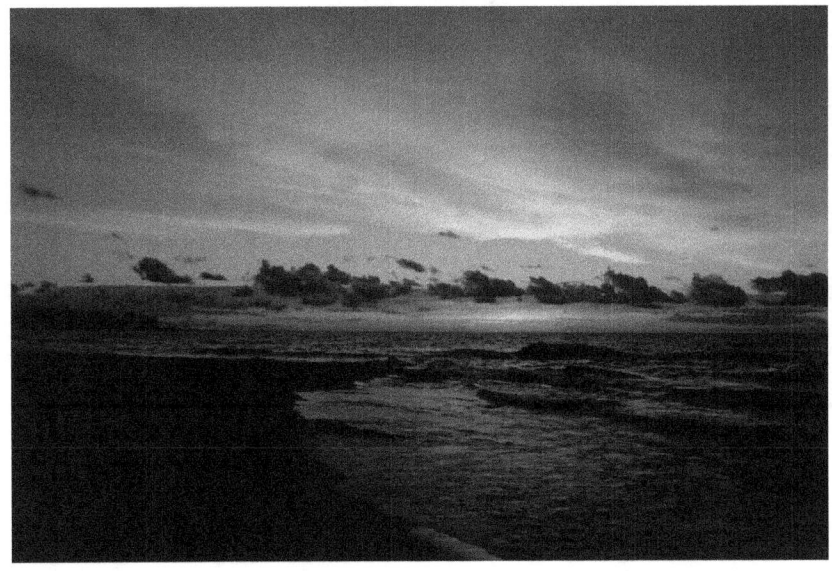

This picture below is one I took because the colors are so vibrant. I stopped on the side of the road and took this picture because the colors were awesome. This was a cloud shot because I had no setup time.

It is still a shot worth taking because of the colors. But if I would have had time would have taken it from a different perspective. 3 or 4 minutes and it would have been too late.

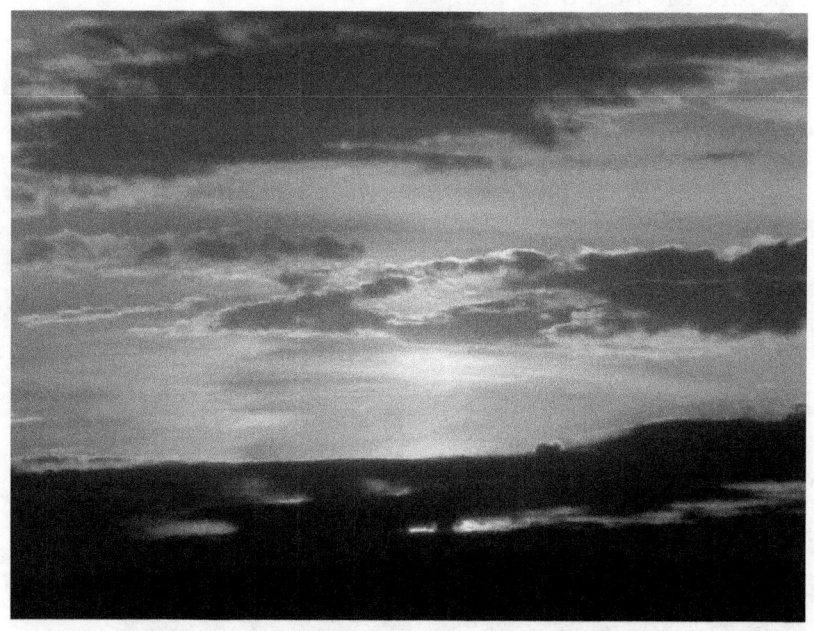

Blur the foreground.

Blurring the foreground of a shot is something you will use as a technique to focus about a shot. Most landscape pictures are not this way. Most landscape photos you want to have sharpness from front to back of the shot.

It takes creativity to find the right subjects to use in a shot where you want to blur the foreground. Most of these shots will be shots you have a limited focus area. You want the foreground blurred to have color. Something to frame the shot to make the viewer look up when they look to the lower part of the picture.

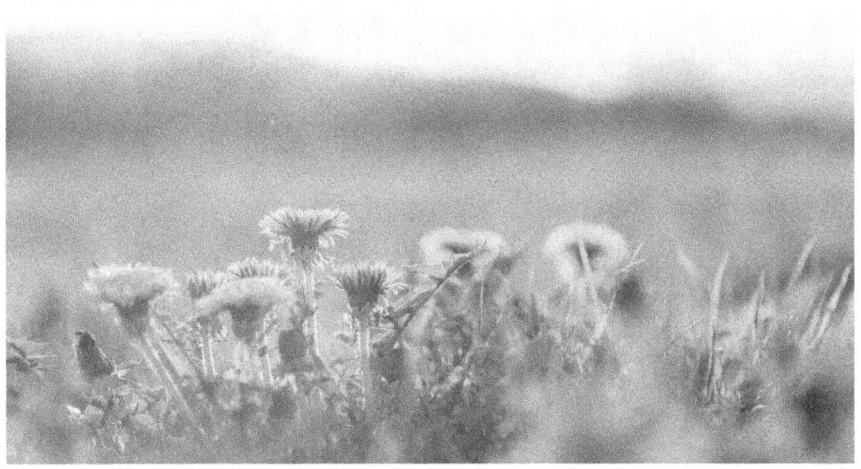

This shot I use the blurring of the foreground as a frame for the subject of the picture. The depth of field view in this shot is narrow. The blur is all around the subject to focus the viewer on the subject.

In this photo, the focus is on the complimentary colors of the yellow and purple flowers. Having the photo blurred all around the focus pulls your eyes right to what I want you to see. Being able to see the purple in the foreground adds to the rest of the shot with extra color.

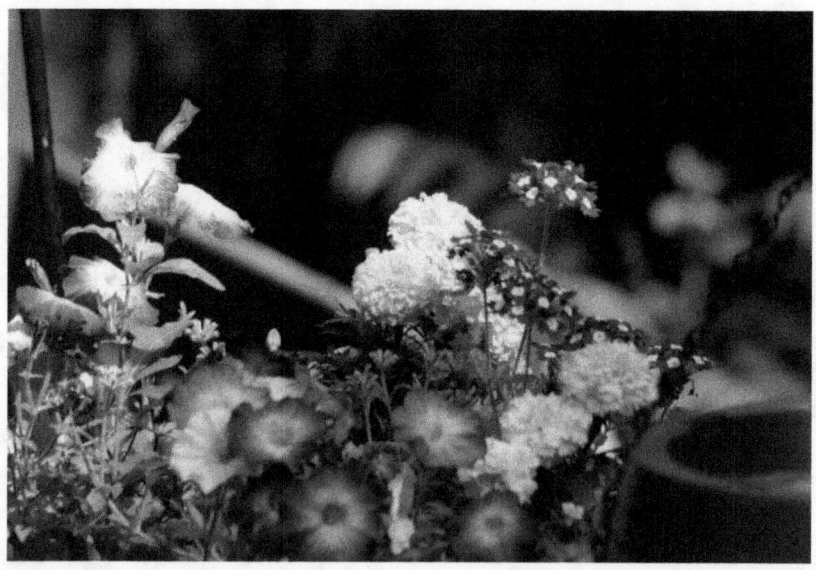

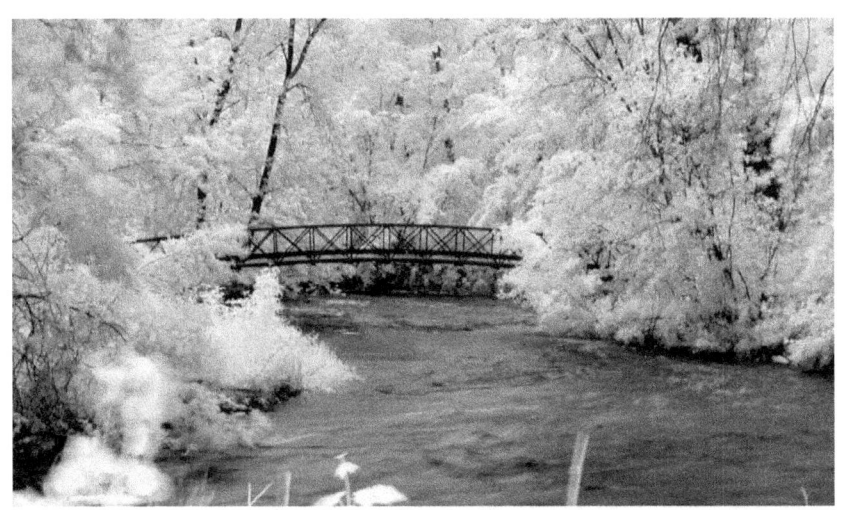

This infrared picture has the foreground blurred to draw your eyes to the bridge. The bridge and the river are the focus of the shot. I love to make infrared pictures. Infrared is so different. It makes things look unique in a way that is not natural, but you still know what it is, and it looks cool.

The next shot has the foreground blurred. This is to make you look to the cathedral in the background. The green and flower colors in the foreground add interest to the shot, but do not take away from it.

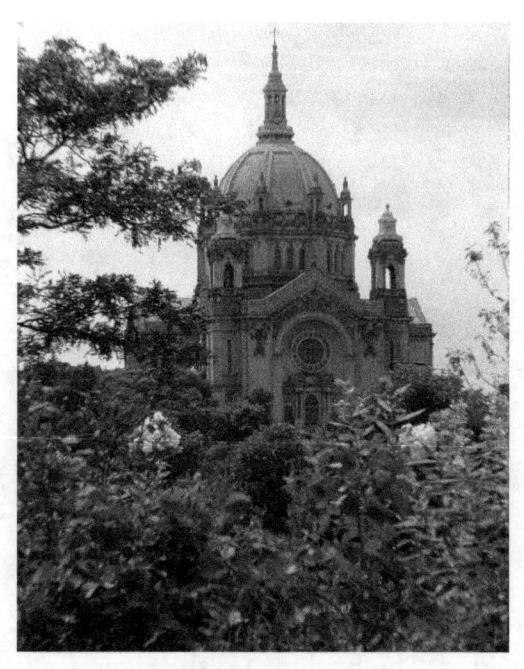

Blur the background.

Blurring the background gives a more focused shot. Same as blurring the foreground. To frame the shot or to direct the viewer's eyes to the subject and the point of the shot.

You can also get cool looking distortion of the background that adds to the picture. It is called bokeh.

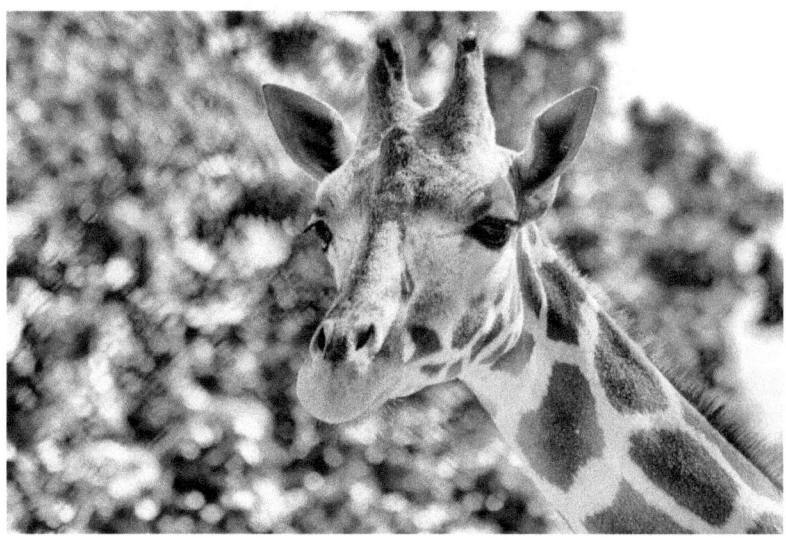

Bokeh is a way you get the effect of the color for interest in the background, without taking away from the subject of the photo. Bokeh also makes the subject jump out of the photo because it makes it super sharp and gives a kind of 3D look to the shot.

Here is a bokeh shot that looks cool because of the background bokeh.

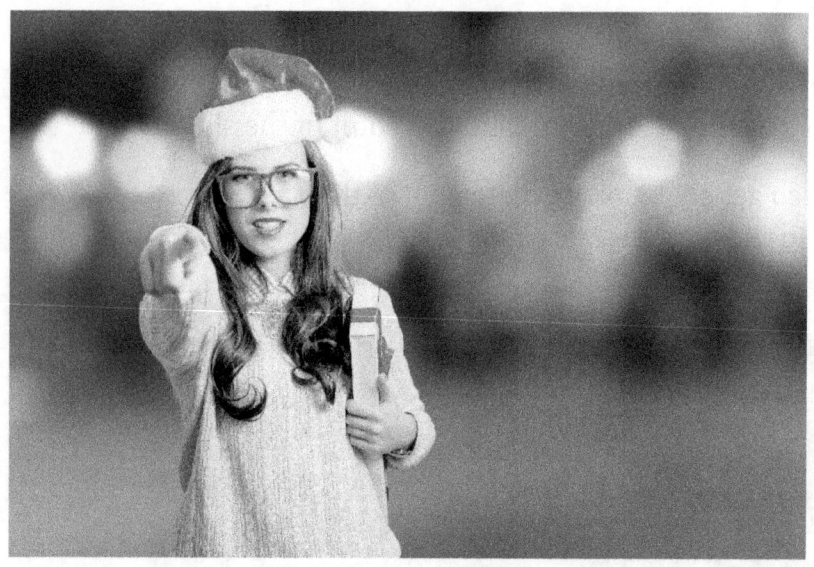

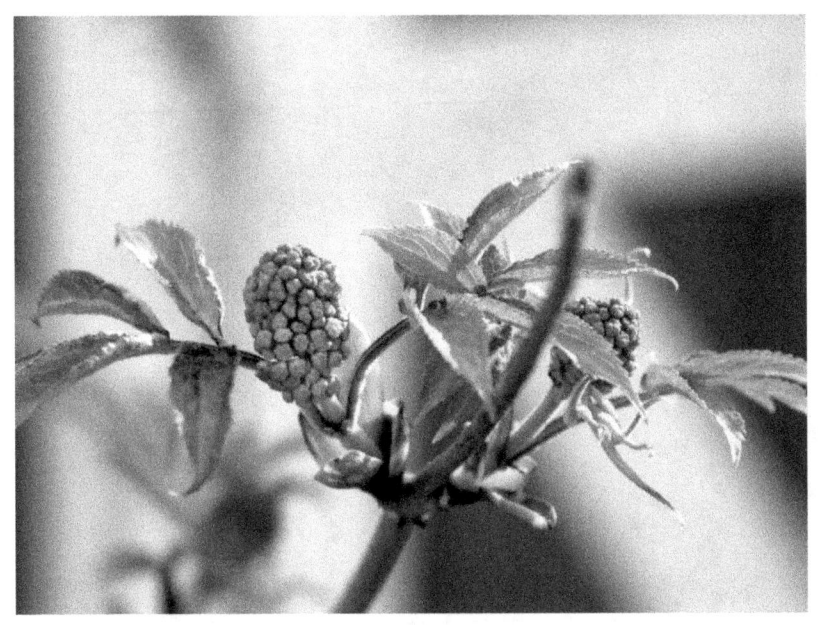

This background blurred by using a macro lens and focusing on the plant. Everything else is out of focus so the viewer knows what the subject is.

A large aperture, small number, such as f2. With a longer focal length can make the area of focus in the shot be small. It can be shallow depth of field. shallow as less than an inch deep.

It makes focusing about your shot more difficult. But you can isolate it and keep everything else out of focus and not distracting.

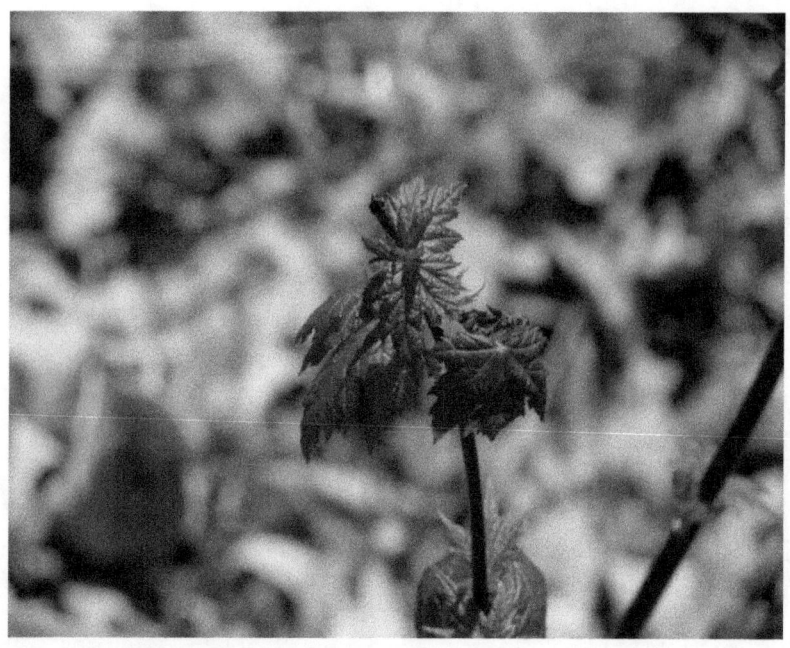

This shot has the background blurred also, so the focus is on the subject only. The background has contrasting colors. So, the red of the tree sprout leaves stand out from the surroundings.

The next two shots are also blurred to make the subject stand out, so they are more visible and more pronounced.

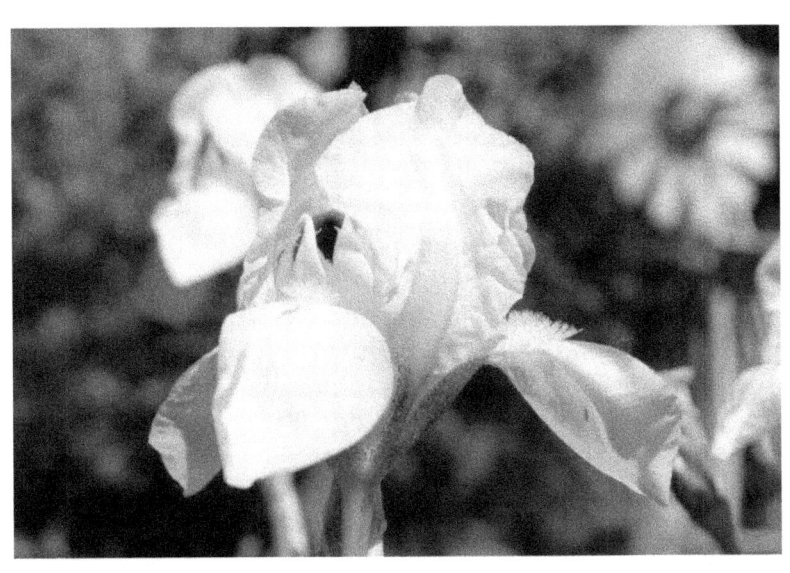

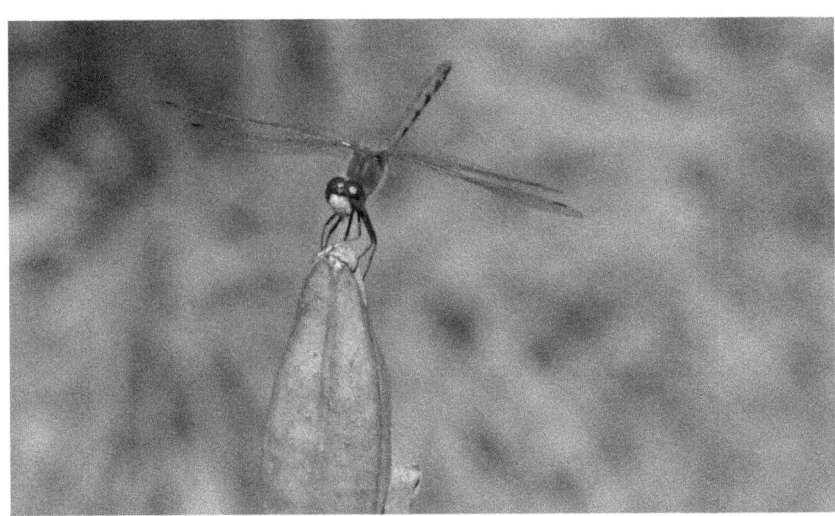

Main Street

This challenge is all about street photography. This is one of my favorite types of photography. What I like so much about street photography is that you have unlimited types of shots you can make.

You can look for and use any subject. From still life's to portraits. I recommend if you take shots of people. You ask them if it is ok. Unless you are taking crowd views or shots where the person is not the subject of focus of the picture. If you want to take portraits for use on a website or some other public display. Get a signed consent form to have permission to use the photos.

Lots of people will think it is cool to have their face on something; it gives them a little feeling of being famous. You can offer to send them a copy of a print if needed to convince them.

I like this shot because it is a nice view of the city of St. Paul. I use the railroad tracks as leading lines to show the view where to look.

The railroad tracks lead the viewer's eyes right to the subject. While adding some interesting objects and perspective to the shot.

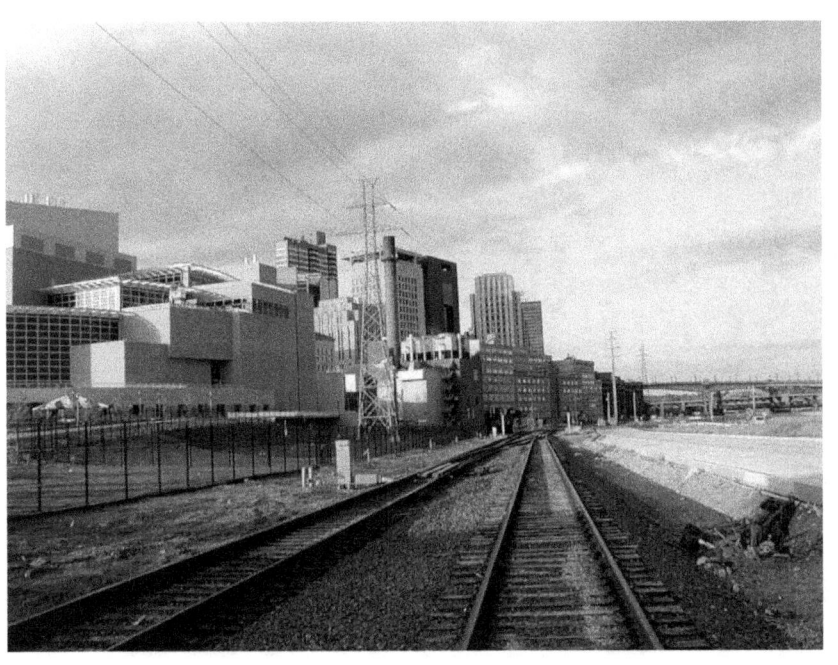

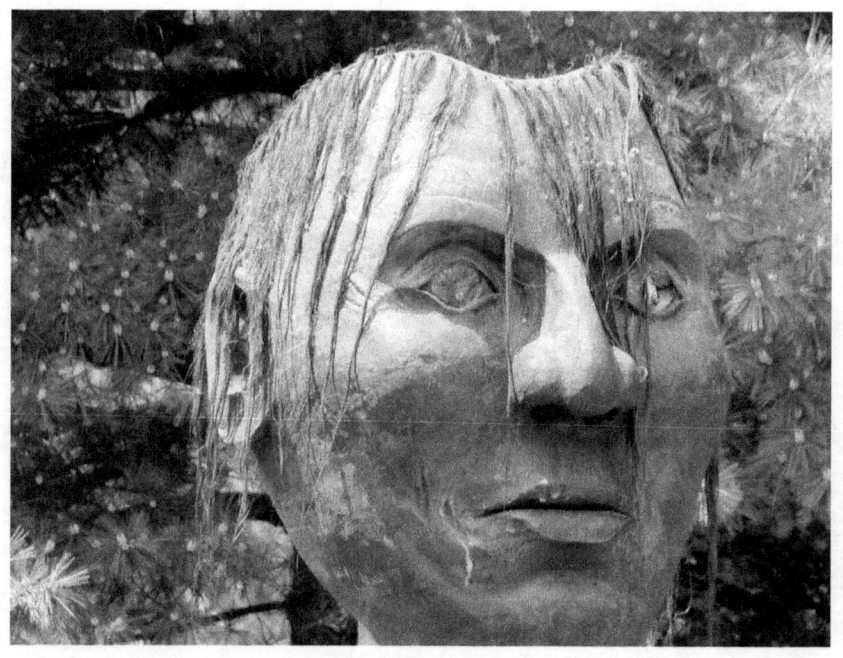

The shot above is a great shot of a sculpture I took at Minnehaha Park in Minneapolis. Not sure what it is, but it looks cool. I made sure that the green from the tree showed through the eyes to add an extra effect to the shot.

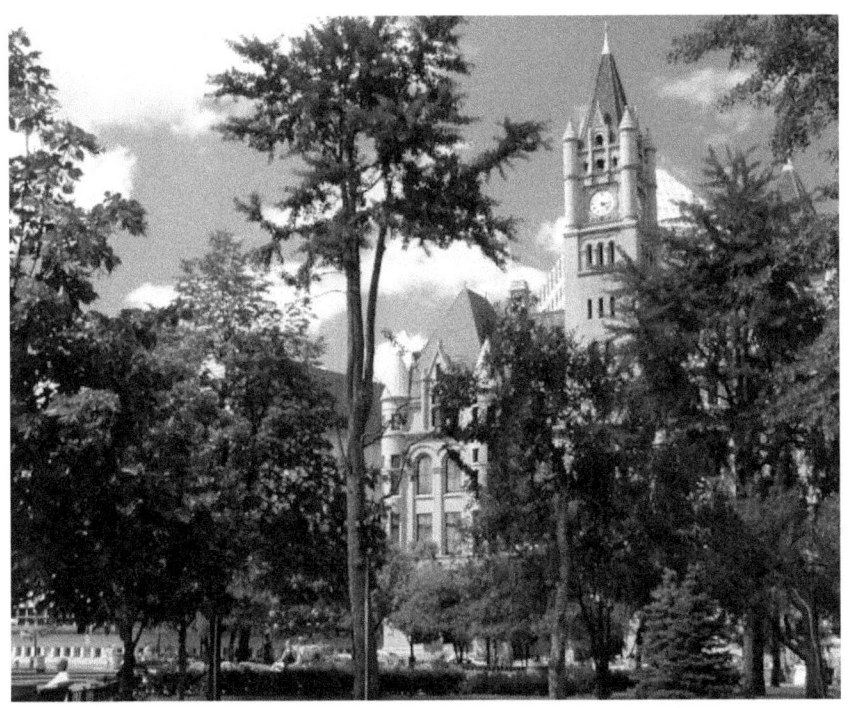

This is a shot from Rice Park in St Paul. The building framed in the background is the Landmark Center. The clock tower framed between the trees with a nice blue sky in the background.

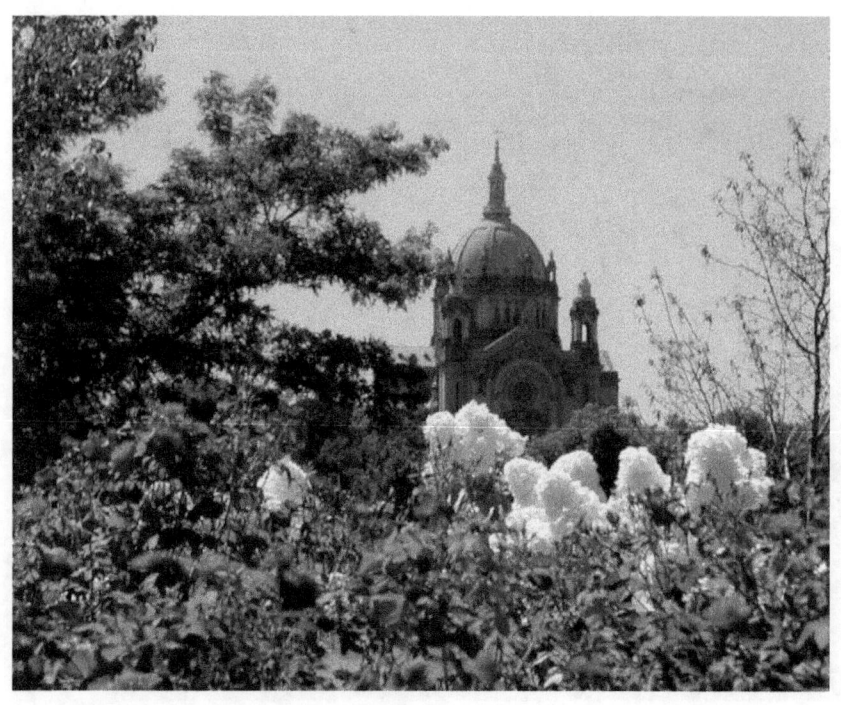

This cool shot is or the St Paul Cathedral. I framed the Cathedral with some great flower blooms and a couple of trees.

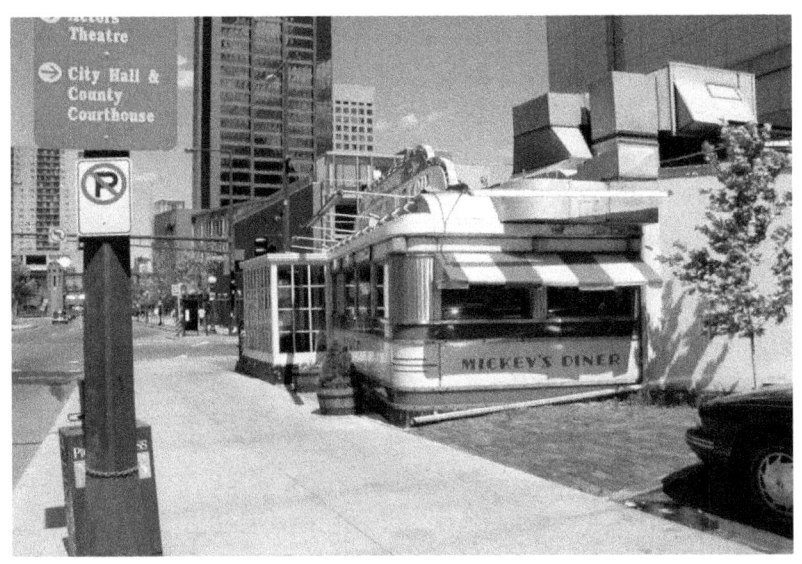

This one is a shot of a landmark in St Paul that many people have seen in movies and couple of music videos.

Street photography can be fun. I have walked around for hours in many places taking shots of anything that looks cool. Many of these shots will also reveal things you did not even see when you snapped the shot.

Parks

Parks are another one of my favorite things to shoot. One of the fun things is that you end up seeing things that most people do not see. I have spent many hours shooting photos at parks.

National parks and many state parks have great subjects to shoot, but do not overlook your local parks. They all offer things that most people never see because they are in a hurry and do not take time to look.

Here is a great shot I took at the park behind my house. It is a great park with 20 miles of trails and some great wildlife. This is all right in the city. This shot was less than 100 yards from my house, and as you can see has great fall colors.

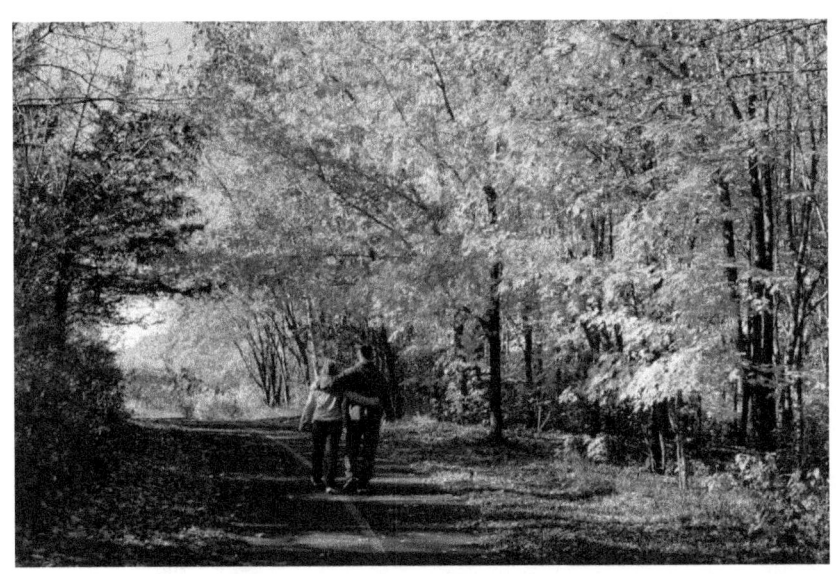

This shot is one I took at Como Park in St Paul Minnesota. Como park is one of the most beautiful parks I have seen anywhere.

 I have spent hundreds of hours at this park taking pictures of everything from flowers to animals at the zoo, to water features, to boats on the lake, to golfers on the golf course. If you are in Minnesota, you need to take a day and check this park out.

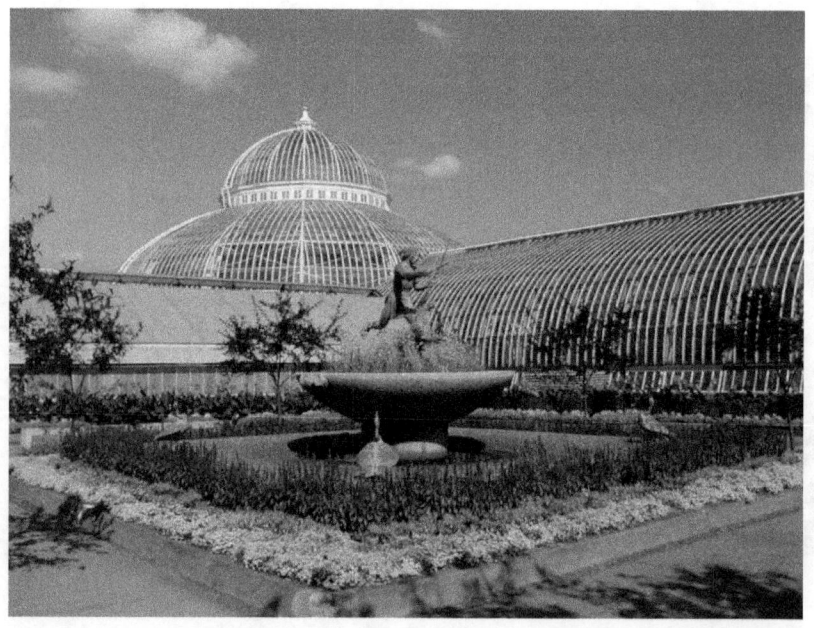

They redid this part several years ago. This garden does not exist anymore. I am so glad I got a great shot of this. I have many pictures of the bronze statue. From different angles and distance.

I do not know where the statue went after the remodel. There are several statues that have disappeared over the years. Ones I have not seen again, but I have taken great shots of them.

This next shot is from the Japanese garden. It is on the other side of the building in the picture above. There are several water features in the garden that make great shots and are worth seeing. These are the things to look for when shooting parks and the feature in the parks.

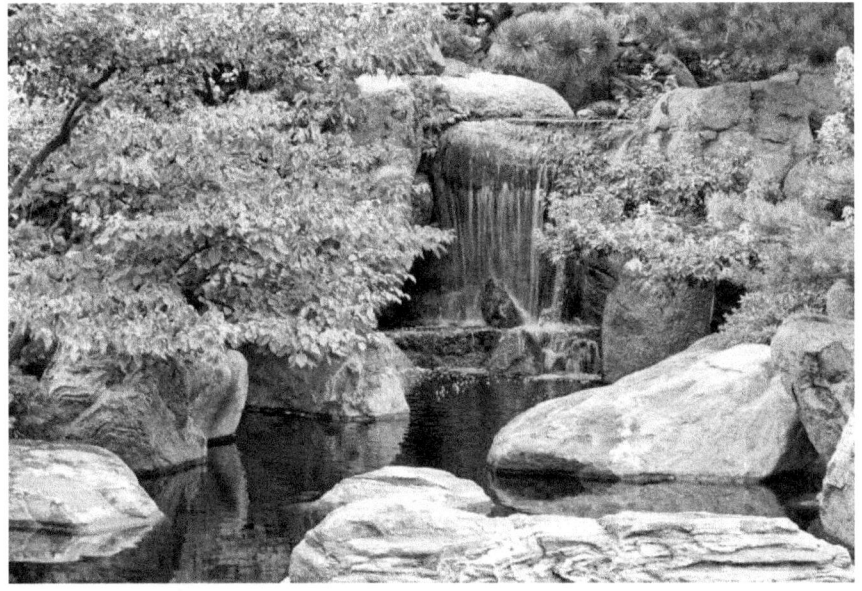

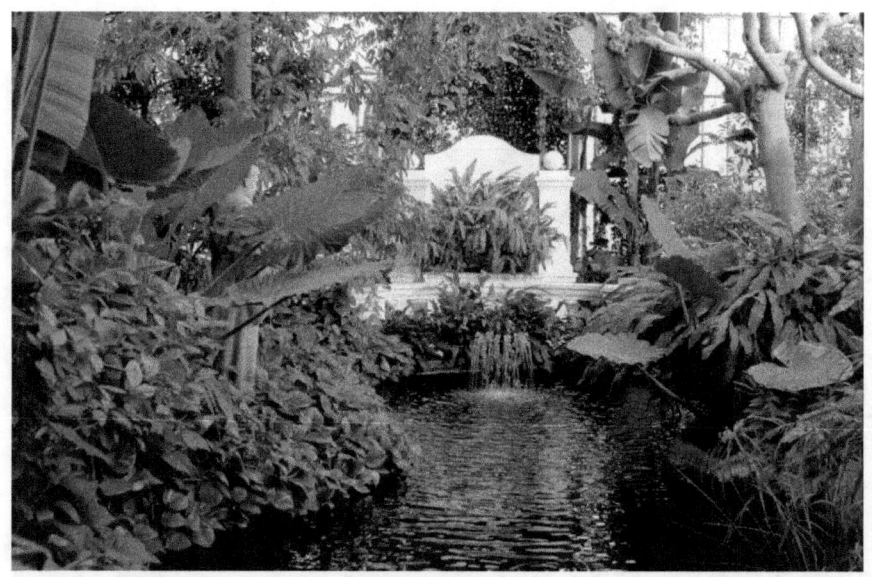

The shot above is inside the building on the other side of the dome in the building above at Como Park in St Paul. It is a tropical garden that creates tough photography in the winter.

Keep your camera warm in the car on the way to the park and then keep it inside your coat next to your body until you get inside the building. If you do not, it takes 20 minutes to get the fog to dry off your lens, so your camera is usable.

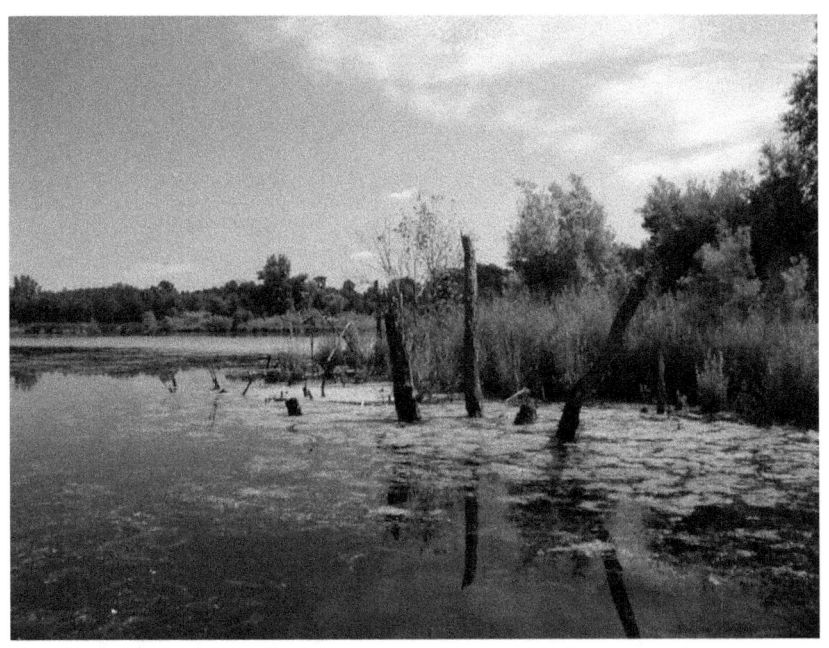

This park is a nature center. It is a great, fun place to walk through. I have spent hundreds of hours taking shots at this park.

It is fun taking pictures of people, but there is a special feeling you get when you are alone and its quiet and see something cool and beautiful that you can capture in a picture. Something you can enjoy for the rest of your life.

Sometimes you get shots that no one will ever be able to take again because the scenes have changed forever.

Shadows

Shadows can add much interest to photos, they can also ruin a picture, it all depends on how you use them. It is important to make sure they are not in shots you do not want them to be in; they will wreck your shot.

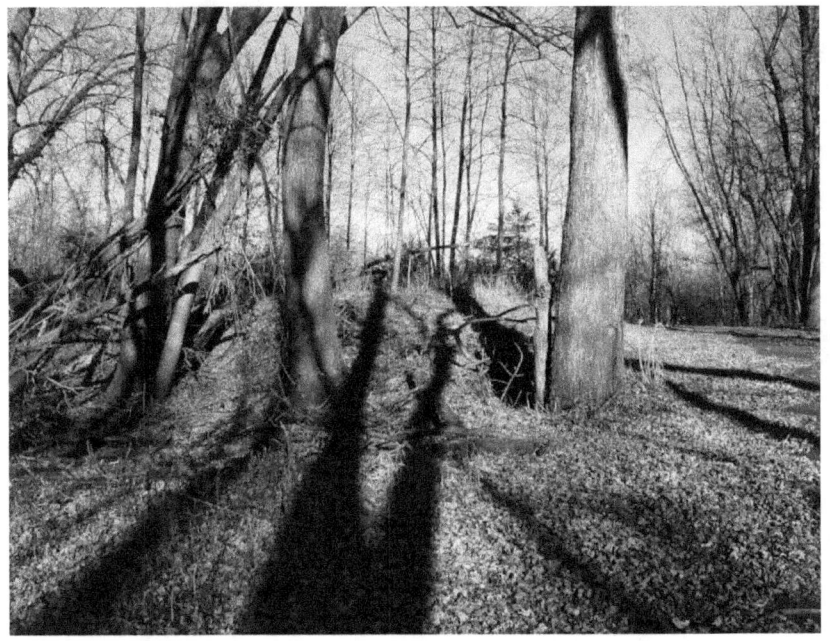

Without the shadows, this shot is boring. With the shadows in the shots, it makes the shot much more interesting, and it makes the shadows the subject of the shot, not just something to enhance the rest of the shot.

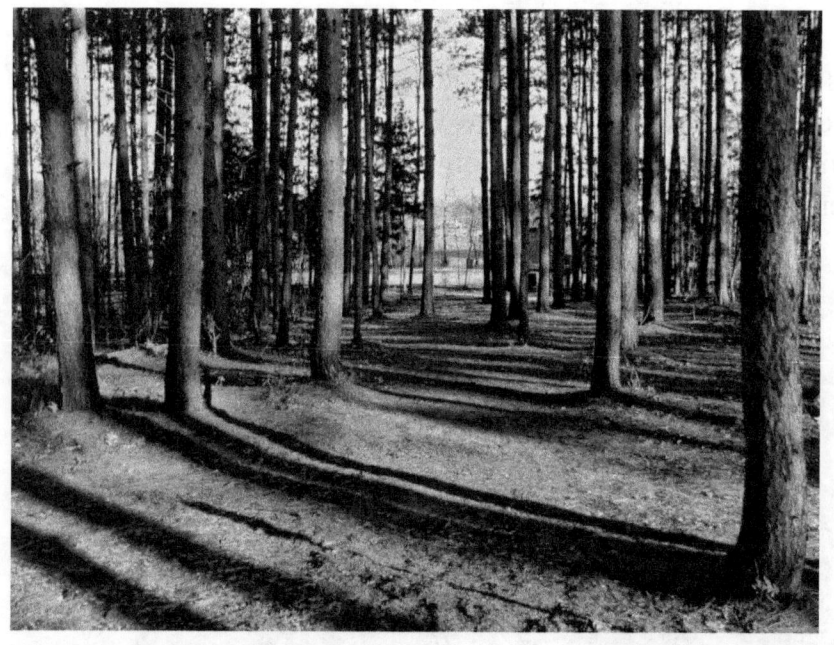

This is another shot that without the shadows it is marginal, the shadows add to the effect of the shot and makes it more interesting.

It adds contrast and tells more of a story. You can see from the shot if you analyze it. The shot is later in the day; the sun is low in the sky because of the long shadows.

There is snow on the ground, so it is winter. The shadows help tell the story of the shot.

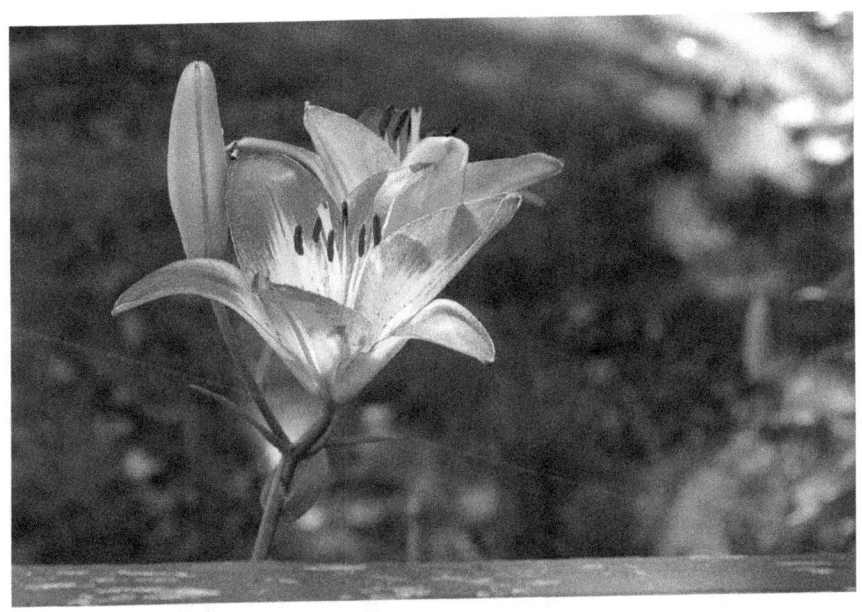

In this shot, I use the shadows in the background to make a darker green background so the colors in the flower pop out. The dark green is a great contrast to the white and pinkish colors of the Lilly.

If the green background were lit with sunlight, the flower would not have the effect of the color. One more shot where I used the shadows, the shadows in this shot are inside the flower to add more of a contrast and make the shot more interesting.

I took this shot in bright harsh sunlight in the middle of the day. I made this shot because the shadows make it not look like harsh midday sun.

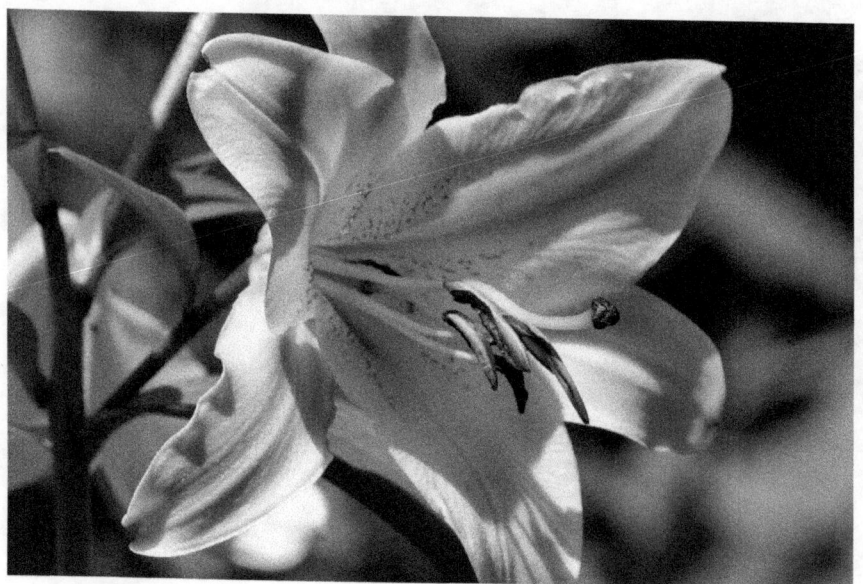

Leading Lines

Leading lines are when you use something else in the foreground of the shot to lead the viewer's eyes to the subject of the shot, or even just through the shot to make it a more interesting and a better shot.

The bridge is the actual subject of the shot. I thought it was worth taking the shot because it is old and broken down and falling apart.

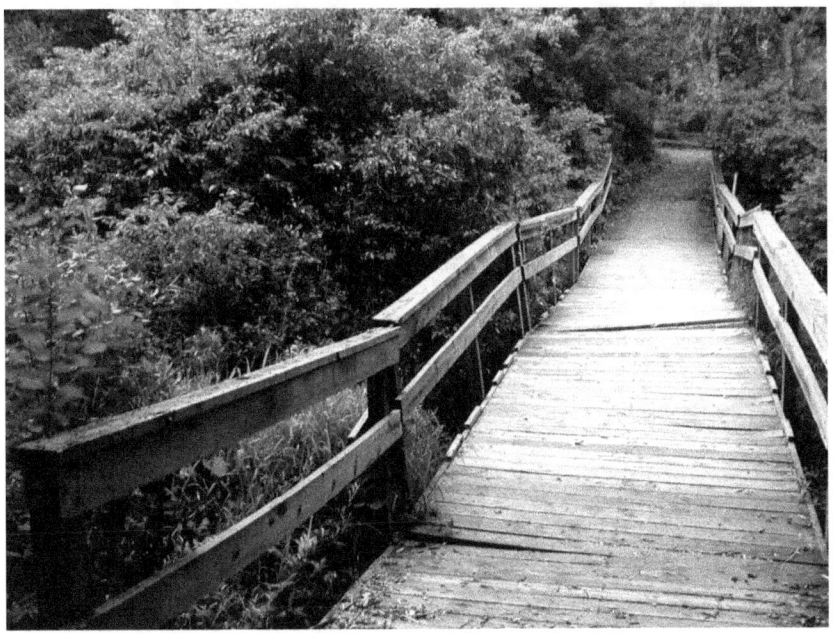

This next shot is of the fountain statue with the sidewalk leading to the subject. It is a cool subject and worth checking out. The wall and the walkway lead you right to the fountain.

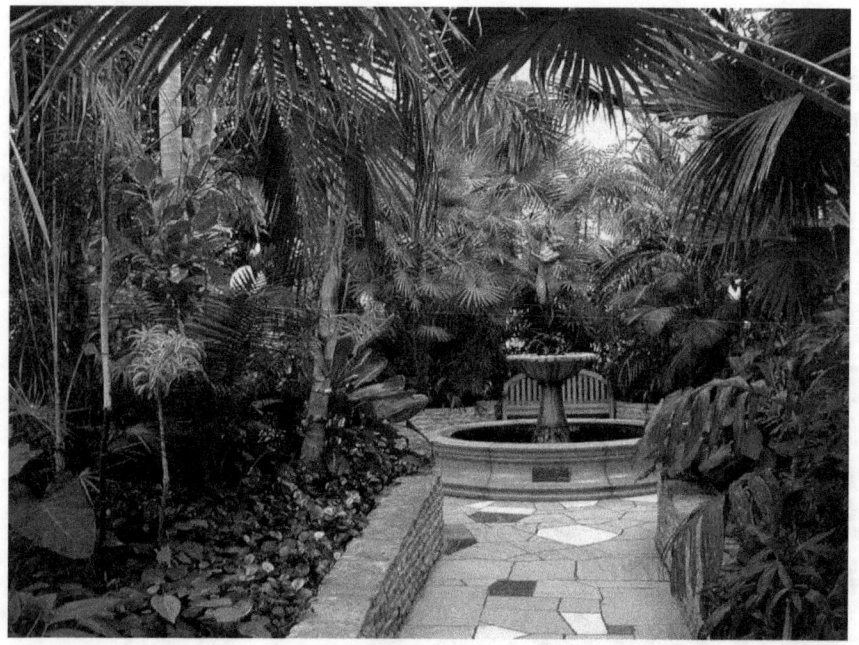

This next shot is of a hole at my favorite disc golf course. The hole is 425 feet long and about 12 feet wide all the way. It is a tough shot because it is so narrow.

The trees on both sides lead you right to the basket.

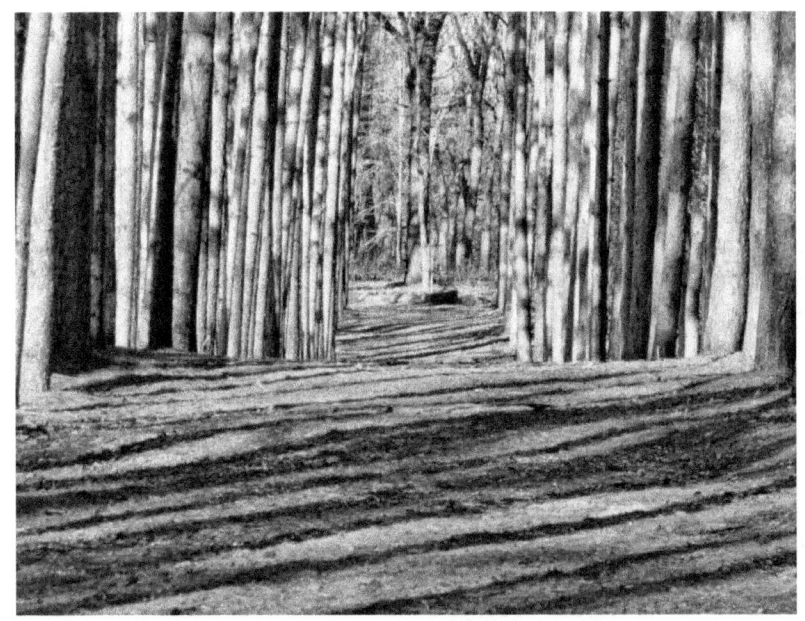

This shot is down the street in downtown St Paul
Minnesota. The subject is the capital building. The street
leads your eyes right to the building. It looks like the
cathedral is hanging from the light pole.

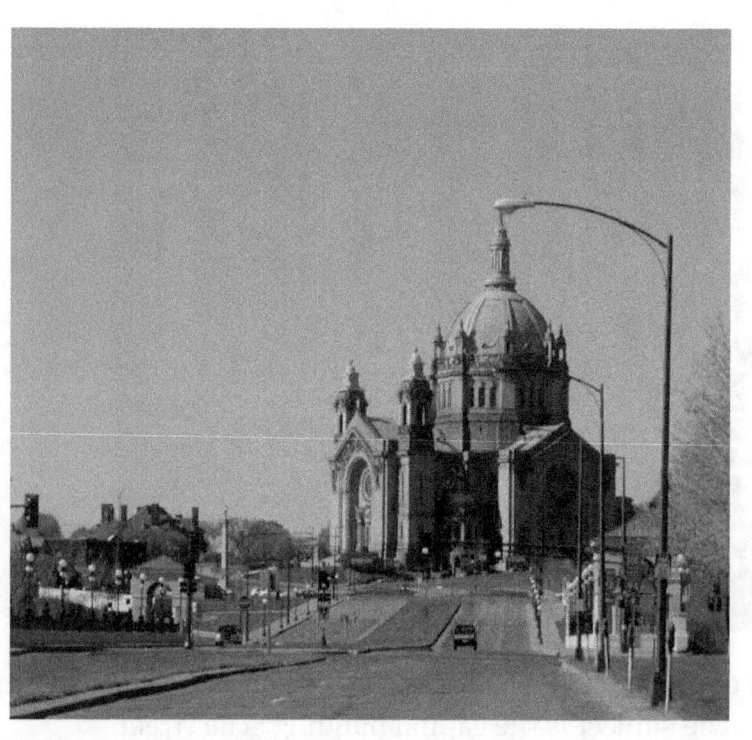

Water

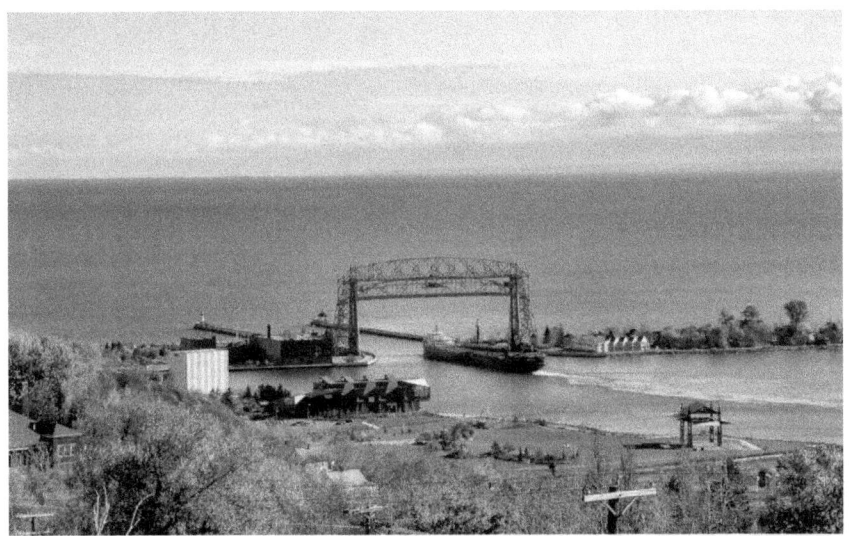

This is a great shot I took from way up on the ridge west of Duluth Minnesota.

It was a great day for taking photos, this area has lots of fog and haze, and you do not get many chances when it is so clear and sunny. The ore ship going under the lift bridge while I was up on the hill was a perfect accent to the shot.

The next shot is one I took from the shore of Lake Harriet looking at the skyline of Minneapolis. It is another rare look, to get the lake so calm and get such a great reflection of the skyline on the water.

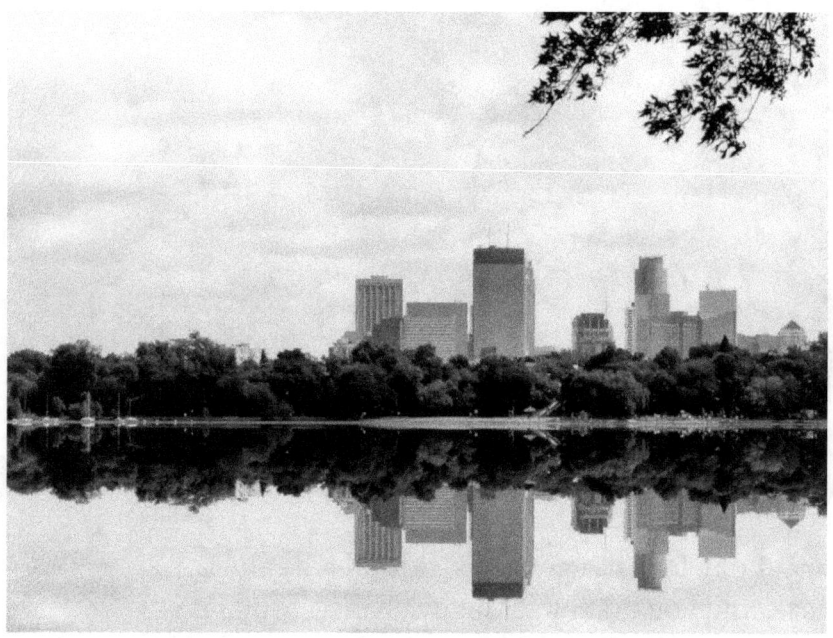

The next shot is from the Boundary waters canoe area wilderness, just after sunset on a beautiful day in late July.

The BWCA wilderness is one of the most relaxing and most well-preserved wilderness areas anywhere. Our last time there, we spent a week there and only say two other groups of people the whole time we were there.

If you can ever get the chance to go there, you should do it.

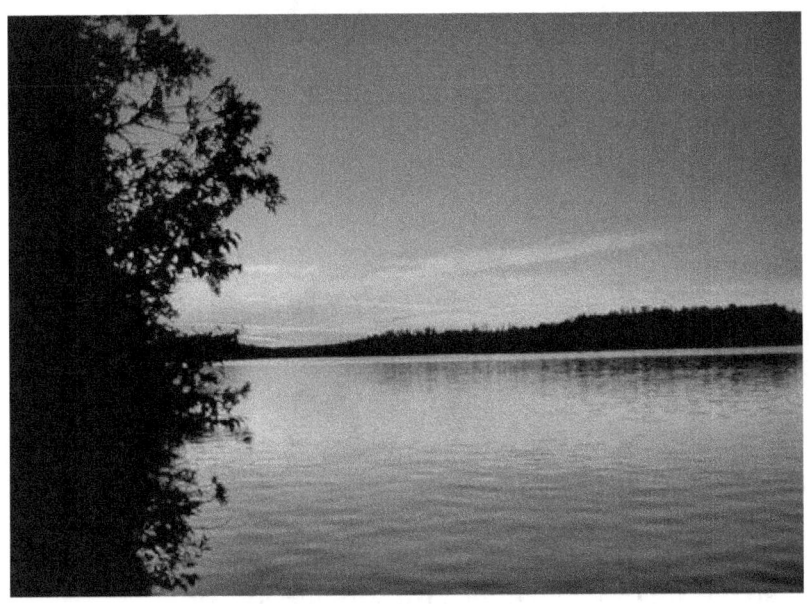

The next shot is one I took on the Kettle river in East Central Minnesota on a beautiful fall day a couple of years ago.

As you can see from most of these shots, the challenge of the photo is water, but the main subject is not the water. The water is a big part of making the photo better.

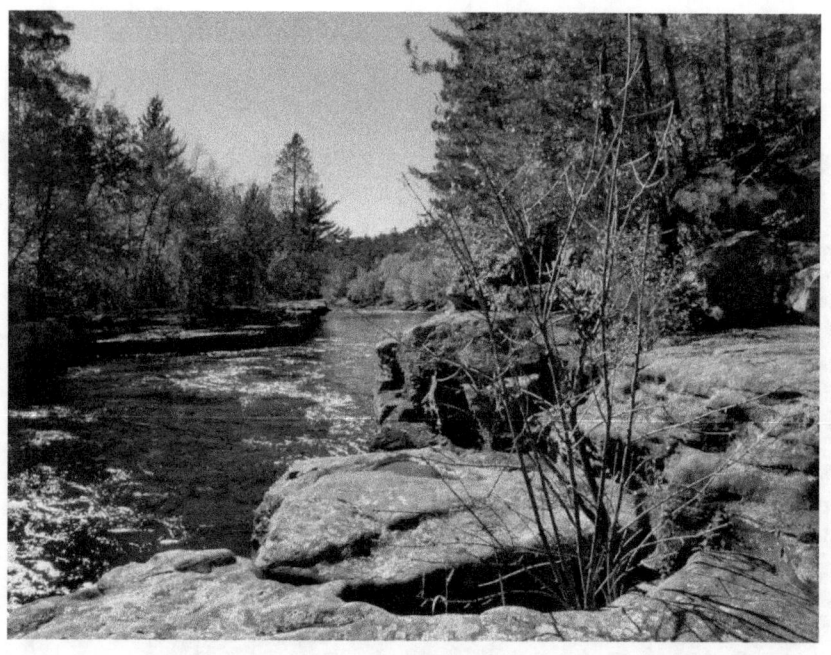

The next shot is another one from Duluth Minnesota. One thing about spending time in Duluth is there are lots of great photo opportunities if you look for them and take advantage of good weather.

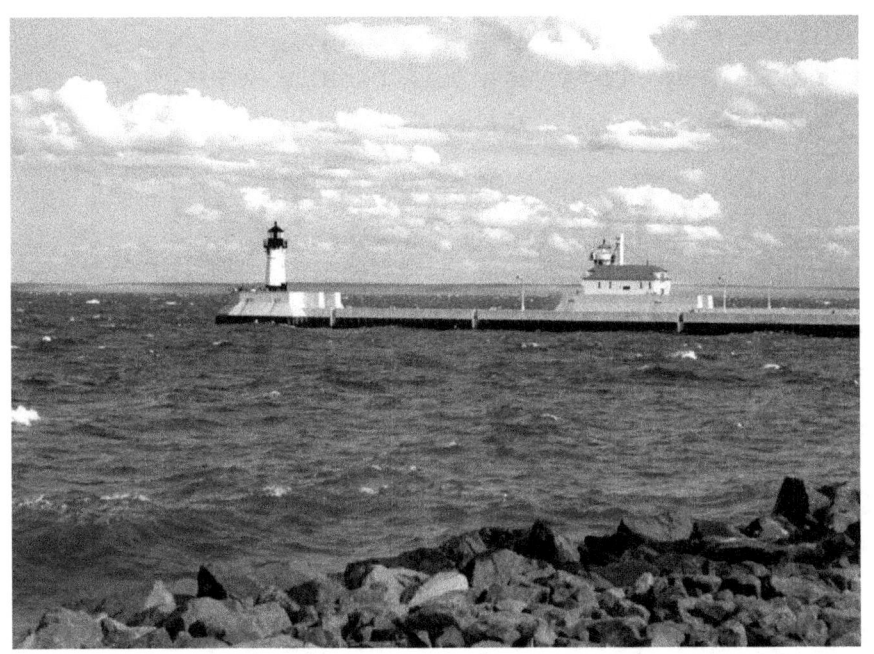

The next shot is a close shot of the water coming over the dam in Anoka Minnesota. It was in bright sunlight with a high shutter speed to freeze the water action.

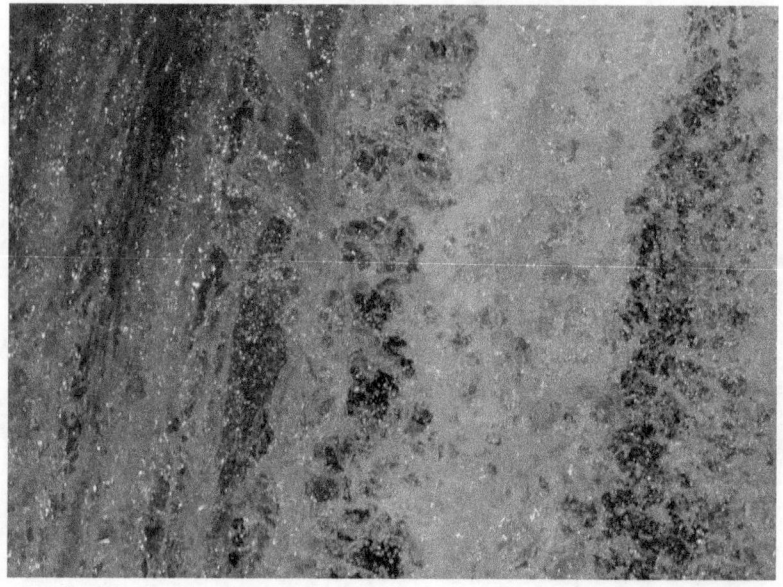

Snow

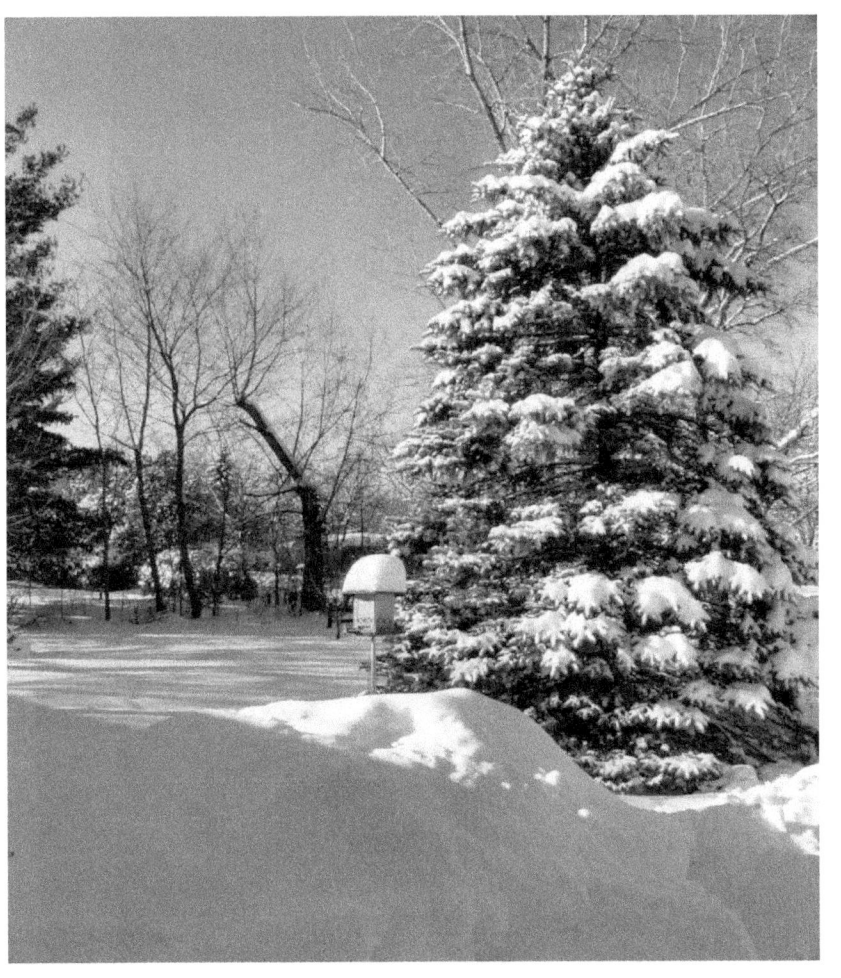

The first shot in this chapter is the morning after a fresh snowfall. Taking shots of snow scenes is sometimes a challenge by itself. It is hard to get your camera meter to get the right exposure and not have the color cast of the blue sky on the snow.

You need to compensate 1.5 to 2 stops to get the right exposure. A huge advantage of digital is you can see the results right away, not like film.

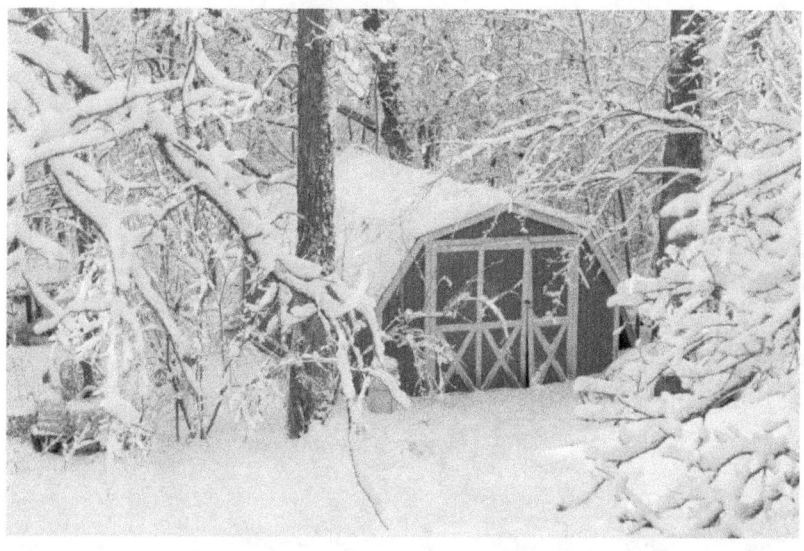

The next shot is off the deck after a nice snow that stuck to the trees. It always looks nice when the snow sticks to the trees, it only lasts for a couple of hours when it happens, so you need to be ready to get the shot.

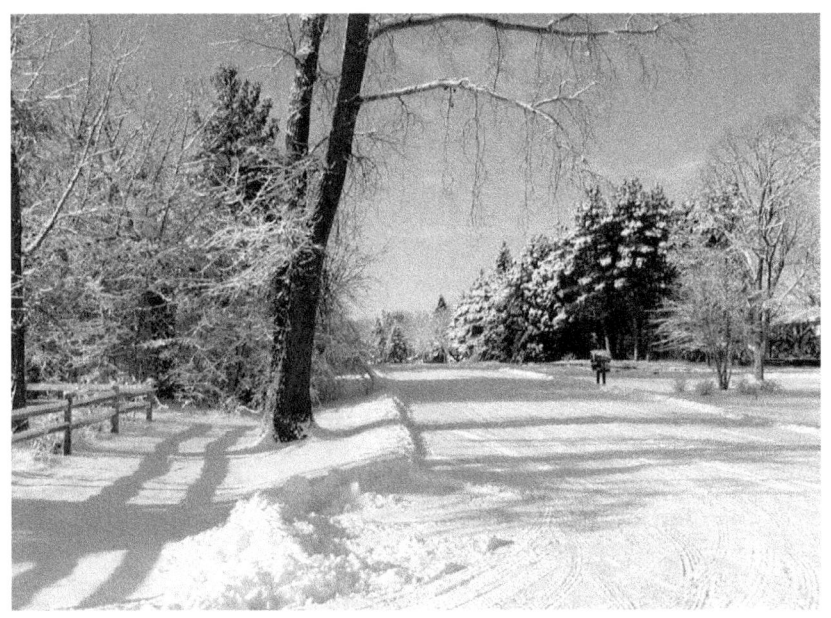

This is a shot down the street from my driveway after another snowstorm. Not a lot of snow but a nice look.

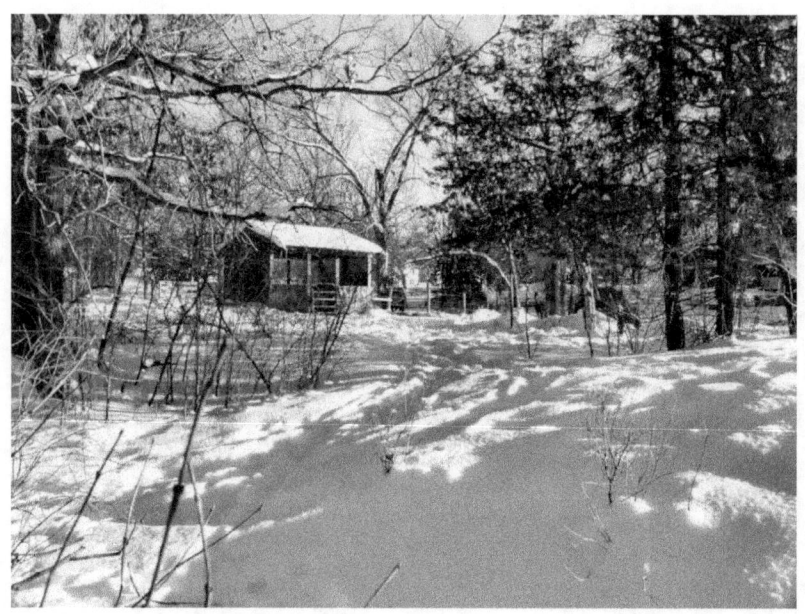

This shot is of the yard of the house behind ours where they raise horses. I spent a lot of time taking shots of the horses and their yard area.

They were so friendly they were sometimes hard to shoot pictures of because they would want to come right to the camera and get a pet.

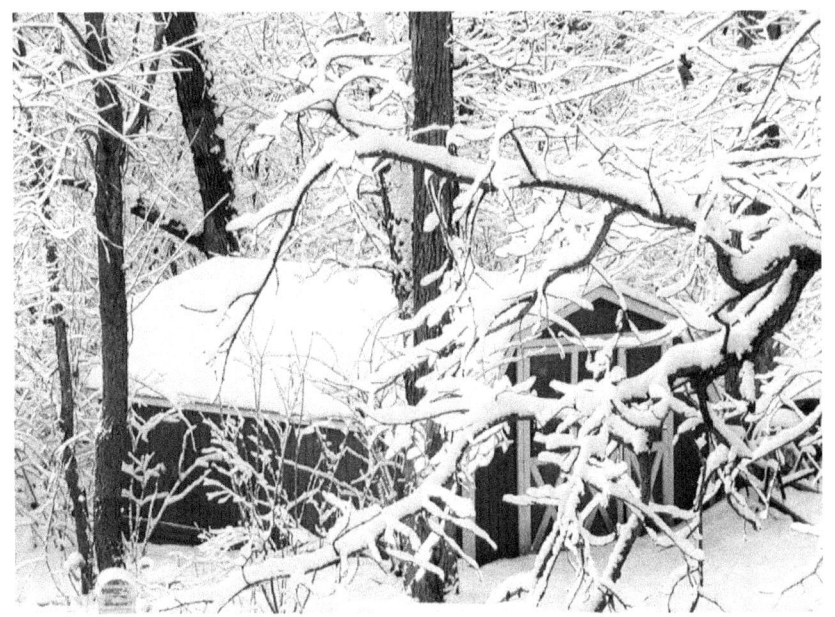

One more day with the snow on the trees from the back
deck after a nice snow cover from the previous night.

Photo walk

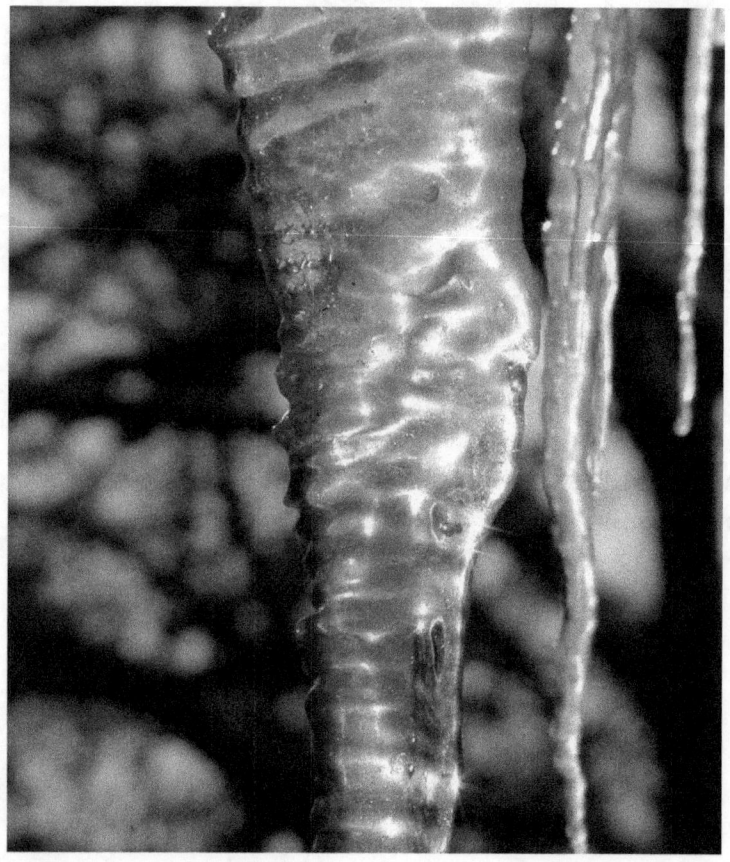

The shot above was such a cool shot because of the way the
light is hitting the ice and it makes it look like it is pewter

or metal, not ice. Vastly different shot I captured just because I was out just walking around with my camera.

This next shot is one I took at the Minnesota state fair a while back. This fountain area does not exist anymore. It is a shot that no one can ever take again.

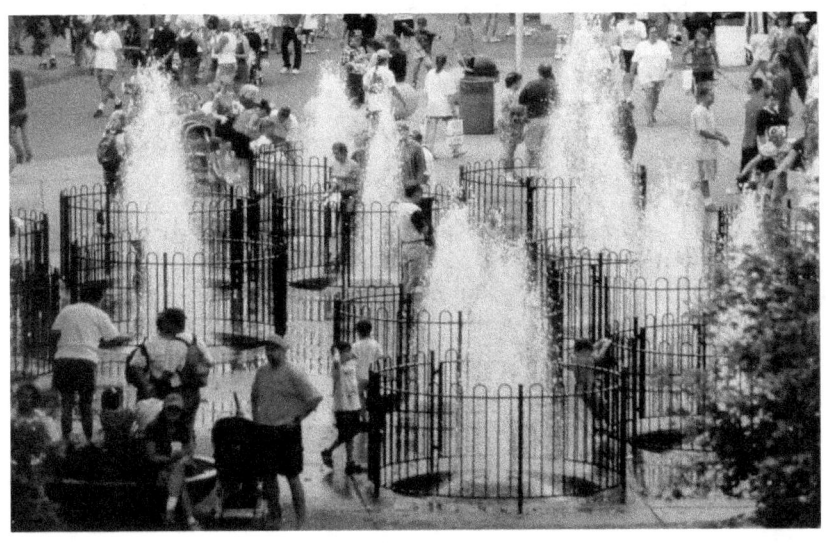

The photo below is a shot of the old Ramsey town hall building.

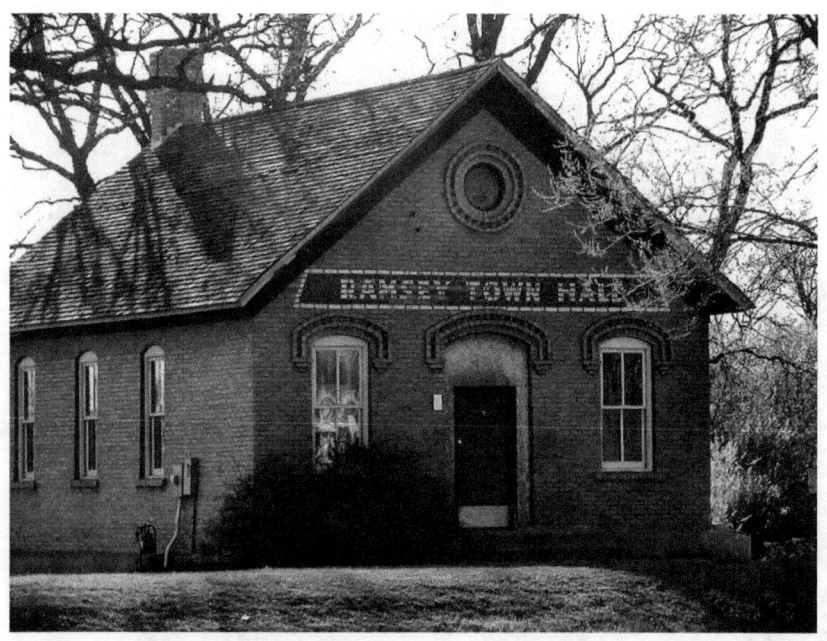

The shot below is one I took on a nice fall day at the dam in Anoka Minnesota. The rum river travels from central Minnesota to Anoka and into the Mississippi river just below this dam.

Every fall they slow the water flow down to just allow a trickle over the dam for the winter. Sometimes in the spring the water is so high, there is just a slight dip as the water goes over the dam.

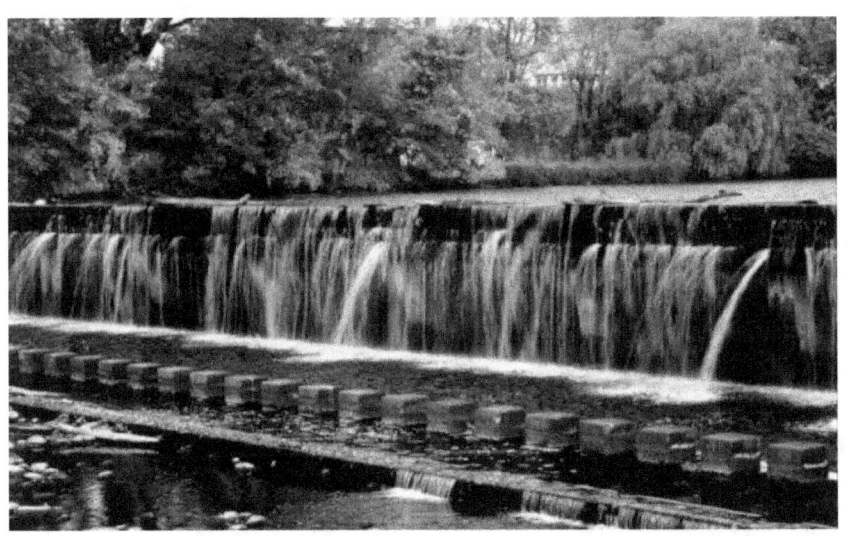

Night Photos

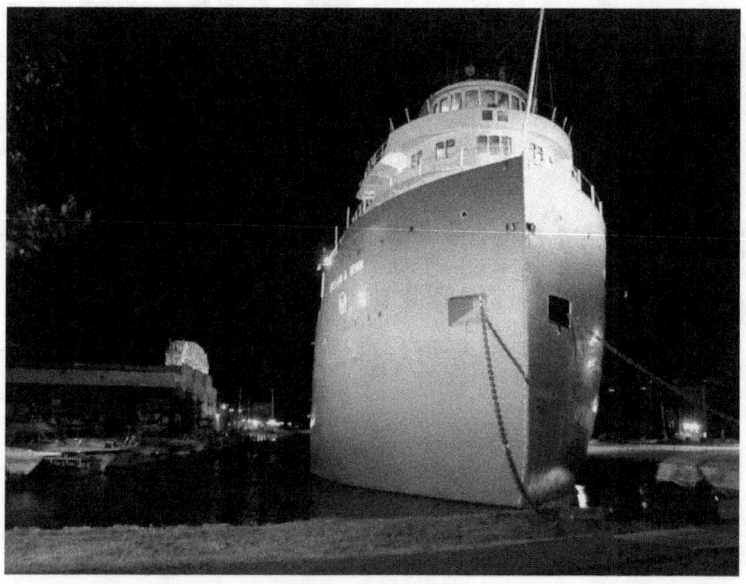

Night photos are fun, but they require a different way of shooting. You can take cool shots at night without a tripod, but it is tough. The long shutter speed requires you to use a higher ISO setting to even have a chance.

This shot from Duluth; I used a tripod for this shot. One problem with using a much higher ISO setting is the noise level in the shot. In the dark areas the noise can make the shot unusable. If you want great shots at night, use a tripod. To get great night shots you need to plan.

The shot below was handheld, no tripod. Try shots handheld, try to lean against something and hold your breath, and squeeze off the shot. Use the highest ISO setting you can and keep the noise down.

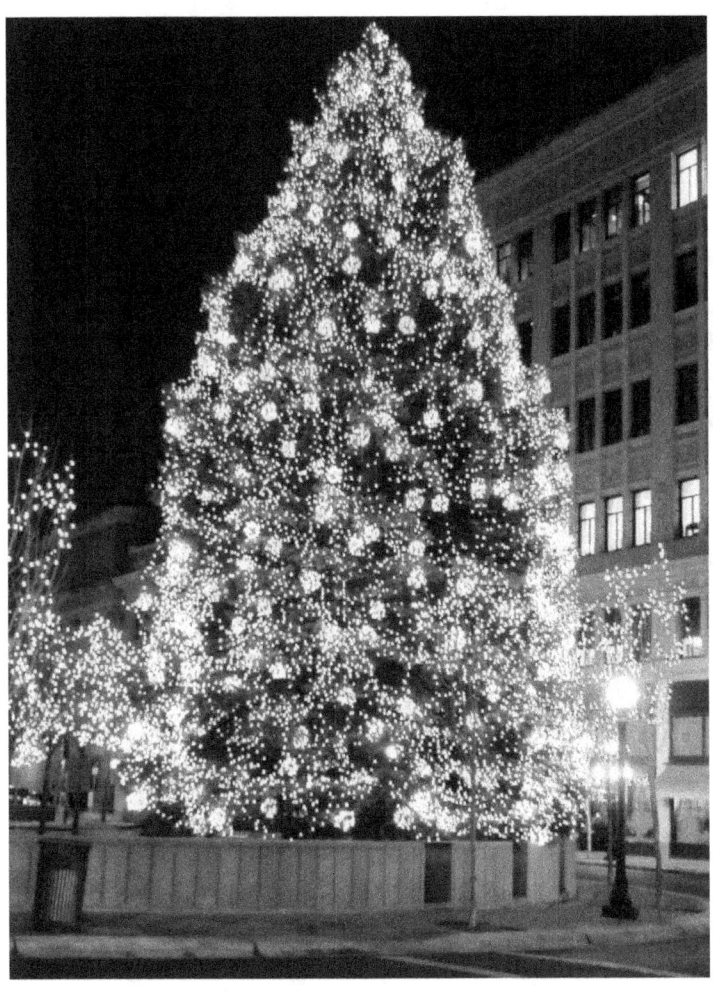

Here is a great way to combine a night shot with a portrait
and a landscape all in one shot.

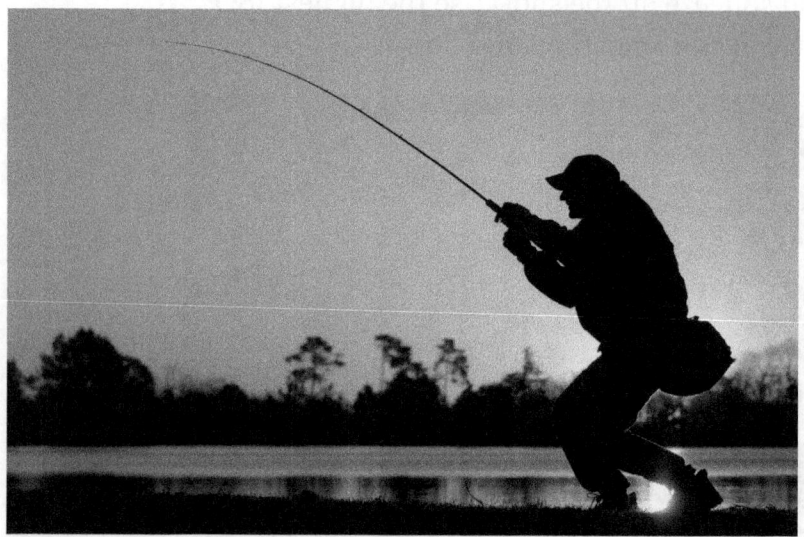

The shot above shows you can take fun shots handheld
with even a point and shoot camera. You need to control
the shutter speed and ISO to get the shutter to stay open
long enough to get the light painting effect.

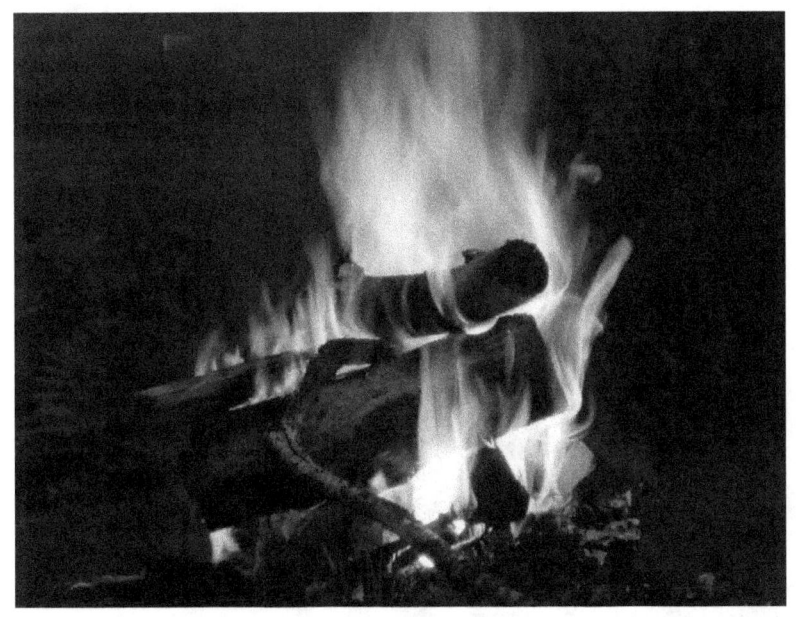

This shot was a handheld shot with my SLR camera and ISO set low to keep the noise down. I think it is a nice fire shot. The key to great night shots with digital cameras, is to take lots of shots. You will get many that you delete, but you can get great shots as well.

Experiment and learn what works and what does not work so well.

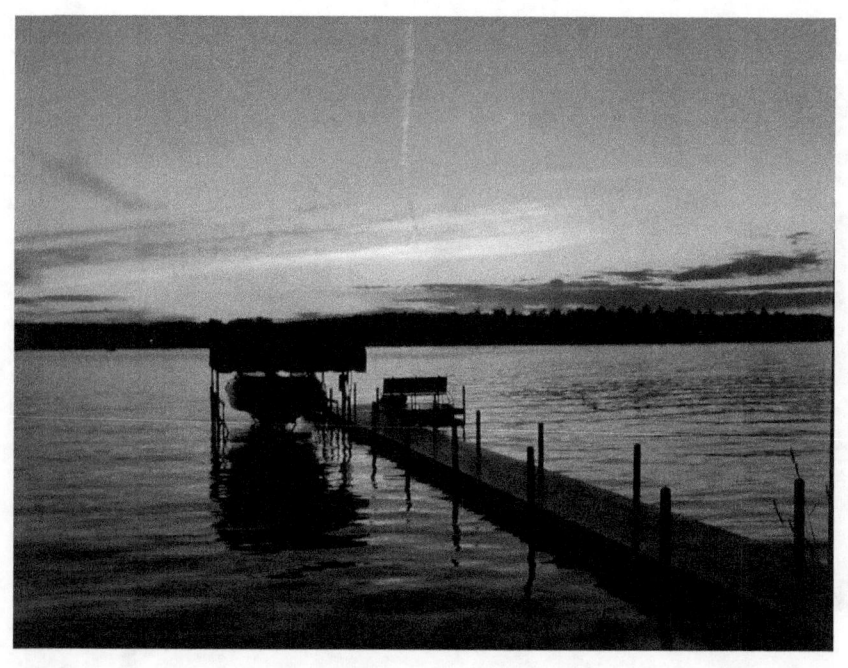

Just a nice peaceful shot from shore, just after sunset.

Pick a theme.

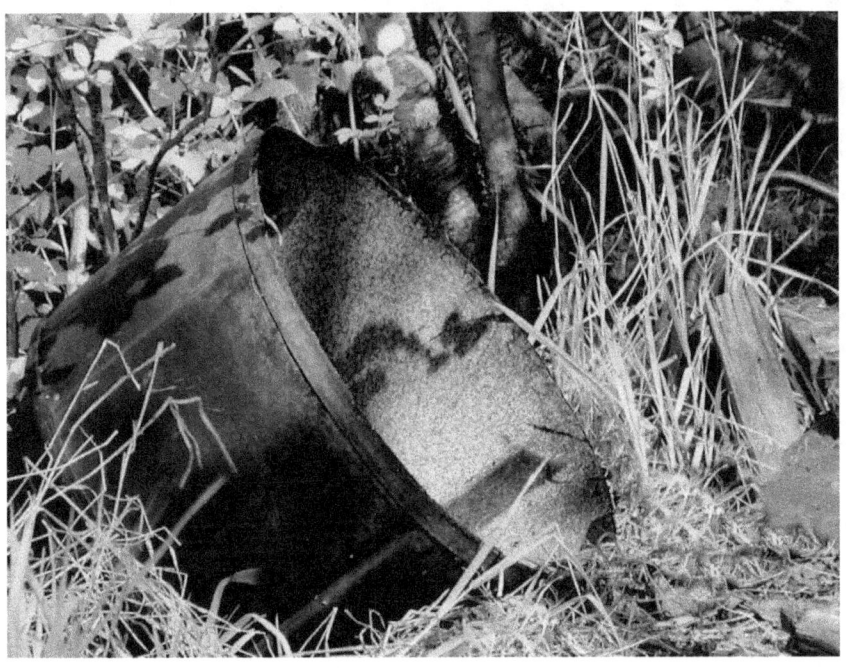

The pick a theme challenge is wide open. The shot above was a theme of Black and White. Some things look better and make a much more interesting photo in black and white than in color. This challenge forces you to look at things in black and white mode, instead of color like normal.

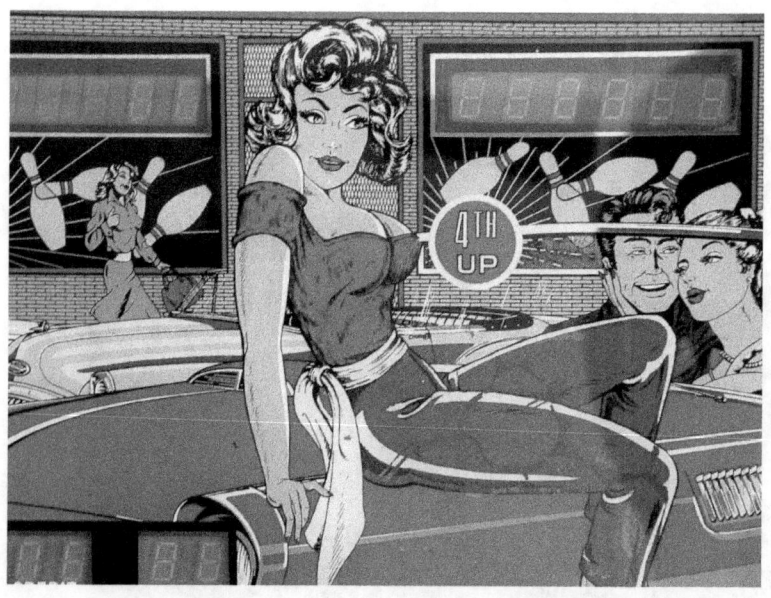

We had three pinball machines in the basement when the kids were growing up. The theme of this is the glass backgrounds of the pinball machines. Taking shots of glass can be challenging.

You will have issues with glare from light off the glass. Change your angles to shoot, side to side and up and down. Look for the best no glare angle, then compose for the shot.

The shot below looks like an easy shot. It took time to get the background setup. It also took time to get the flash set up, so the background was more neutral, and the flash caught the crystal to look like the torch was glowing.

It is the little things that sometime people do not even realize they see. These are the things that can make the shot great.

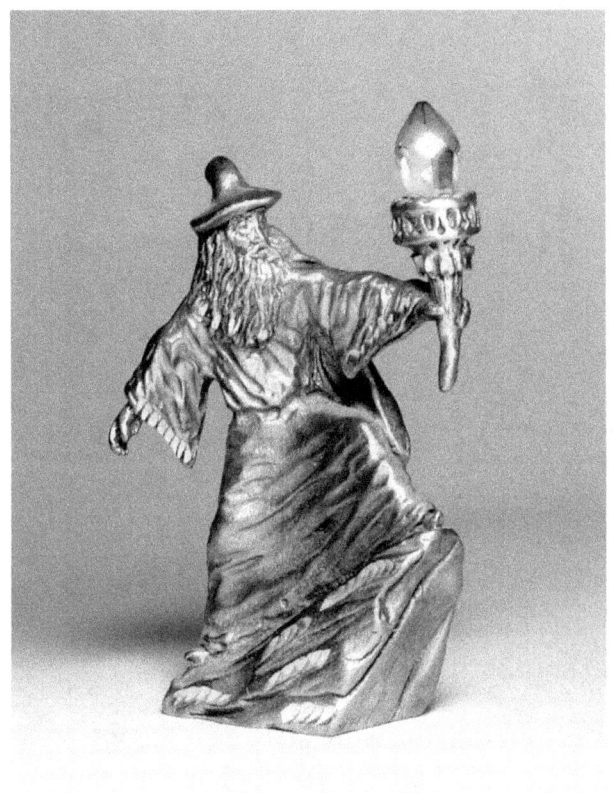

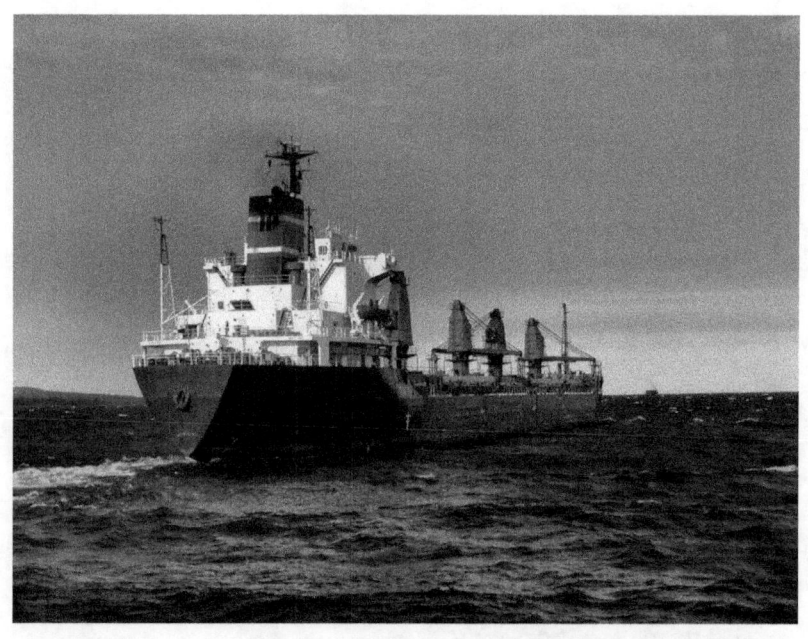

This theme was ships. We were in Duluth. I wanted to make it look like I was out on the Lake with the ships. I took this shot from shore with a good long zoom.

 I got the effect I was looking, for while getting a second ship in the shot with the main one. If you look just to the right of the ship in the foreground, you will see another ship in the distance as they head out to cross Lake Superior.

There are things I have an ongoing challenge to shoot. One of them is planes. I will always stop and take shots of cool

airplanes if the opportunity arises. This is a cool looking
jet parked at the Anoka Co. airport.

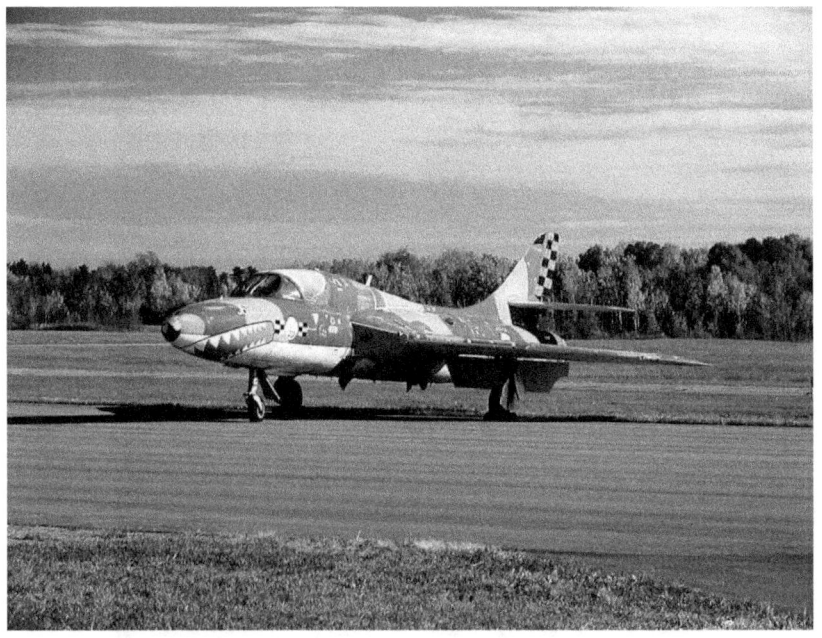

Infrared

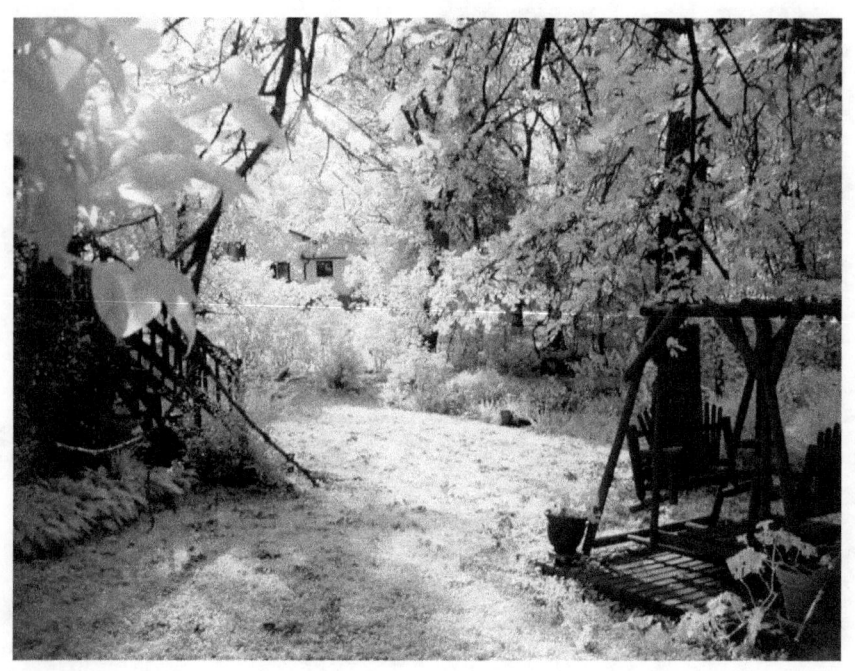

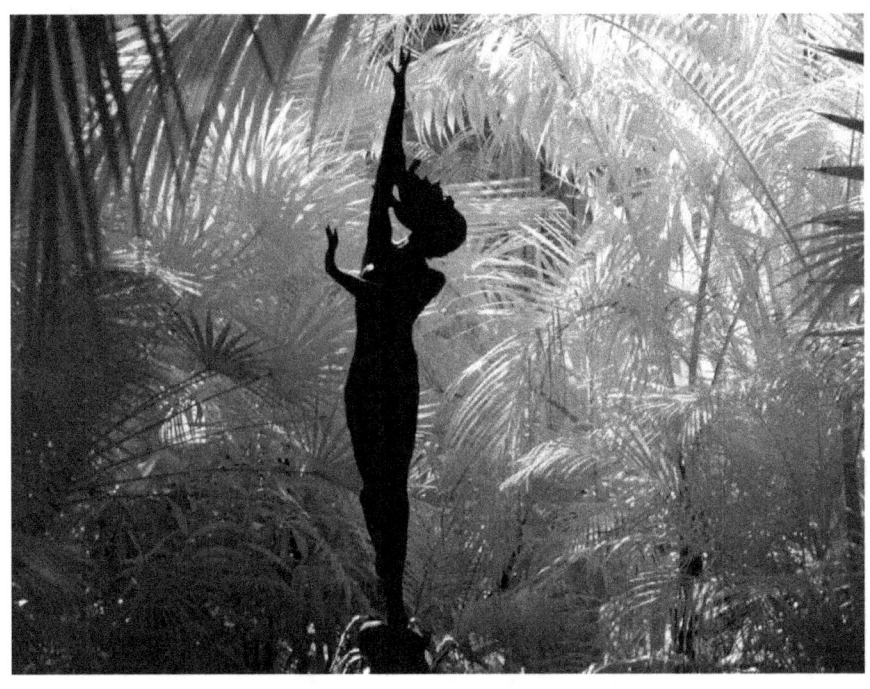

This challenge is one that will take a little more work. You will need a camera that will see infrared light, and a filter to get the great effect. This challenge is easier if you have an all-in-one crossover camera. One with a fixed lens that is not a DSLR. If you have an old camera, you can look for a video on how to take off the filter that makes the camera not see the infrared light.

To check a camera, get an infrared TV or DVD remote. Look through the lens of your camera and point the remote at the camera lens. Push any buttons on the remote. If you see the light flashing when you push the remote, it shows the camera will work for infrared photography.

[Here is a good article about using Infrared filters.](#)

You need bright sunny days for the best infrared. The filters are dark, and you need a lot of light.

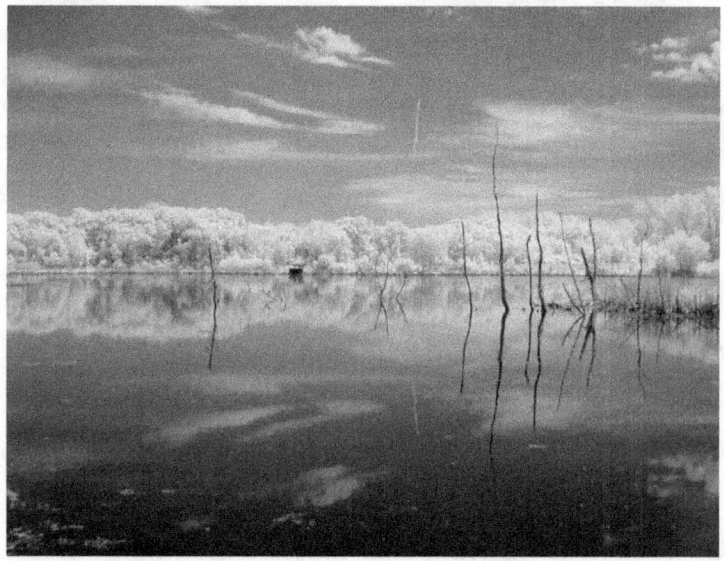

One of the cool things about infrared is that it makes foliage look white, the lighter on the foliage, the whiter it looks.

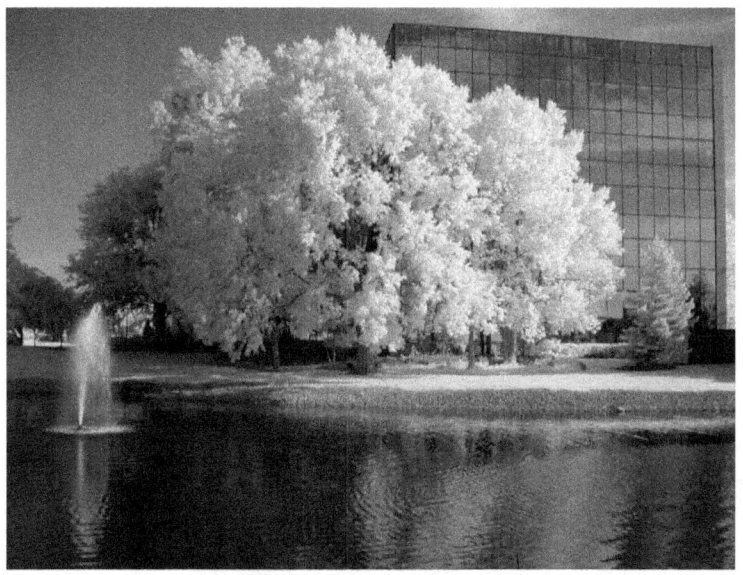

If you convert the shots to black and white, you can get cool black and white shots. Play with it and see for yourself.

These shots were almost all taken with a 2mp Olympus camera, a 2100uz. For a fixed lens long zoom camera, I think it was one of the best built. After 30,000 pictures, it has not worked for a while.

 If I could get a new one now, I would. I took over 30,000 pictures with that camera, and it was perfect for infrared, and all I had to do was screw a filter on the lens it was ready to go.

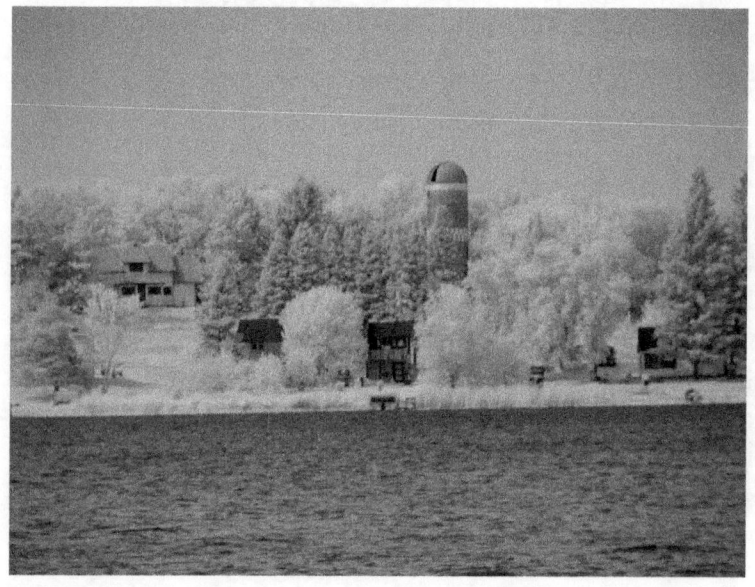

Infrared is such an interesting look, and a lot of fun to experiment with. If you have a camera that will do it, check it out, you will have fun with what you can do.

Repeating Patterns

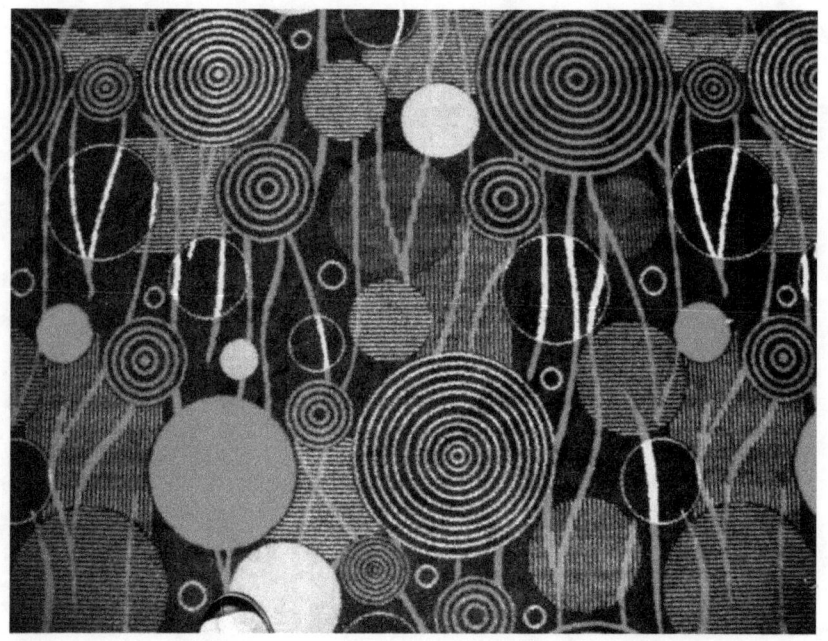

As with most of the challenges, the point is to get you to look at things you would not pay attention too. This shot is a shot of carpet at a doctor's office. I took it with my phone, but I think it is an interesting shot. Can you remember what the carpet at your doctor's office looks like, probable not.

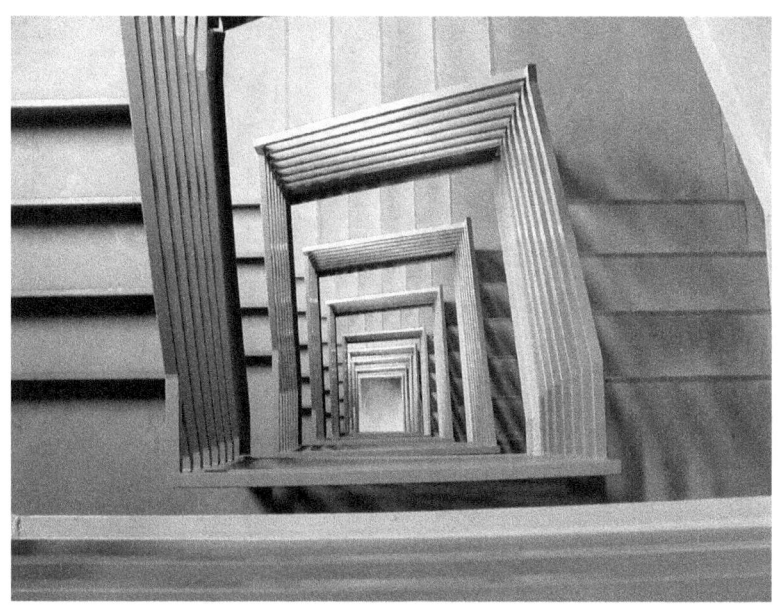

This is a shot down a cool stairwell at my brother-in-law's business. Something you may look at and say cool. But taking a shot and keeping it for future use is even cooler.

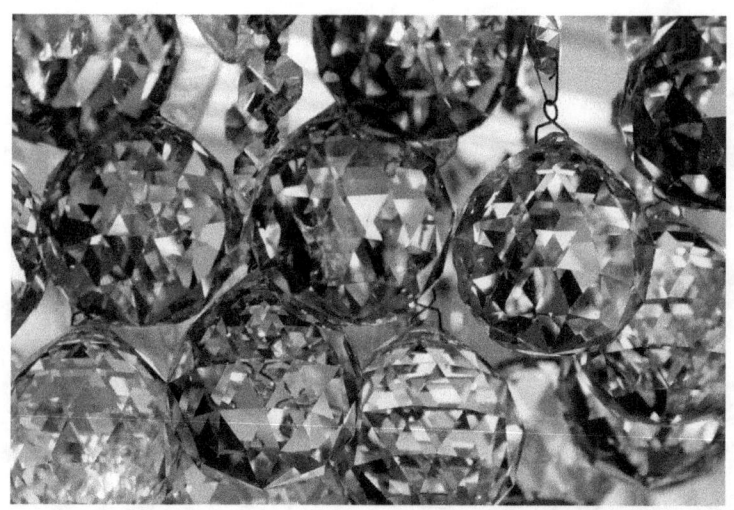

This shot is of a fancy lamp that had golf ball size crystal hanging from the bottom of it. My wife loved it because when the sun came through the window, there were thousands of little rainbows all over the house walls.

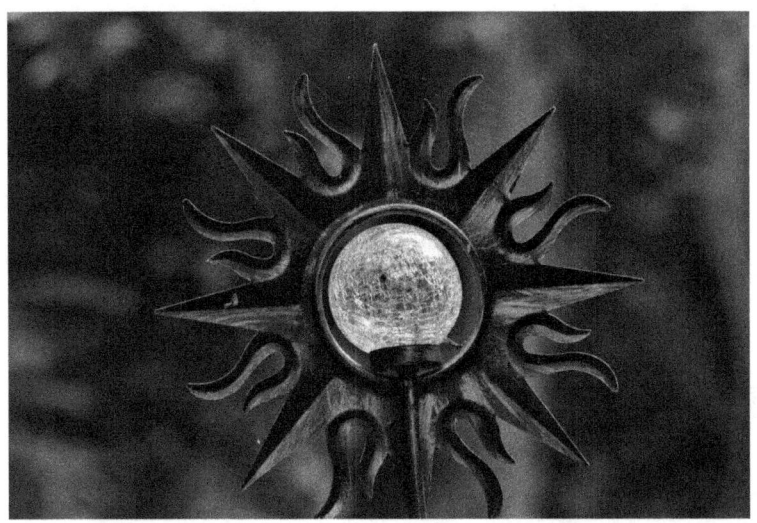

This shot works because of the pattern of the outside of the light, but the glass bulb in the center pulls it all together as a cool shot. This is a solar garden light that stopped working; we kept it for a while even after, just because it looked awesome.

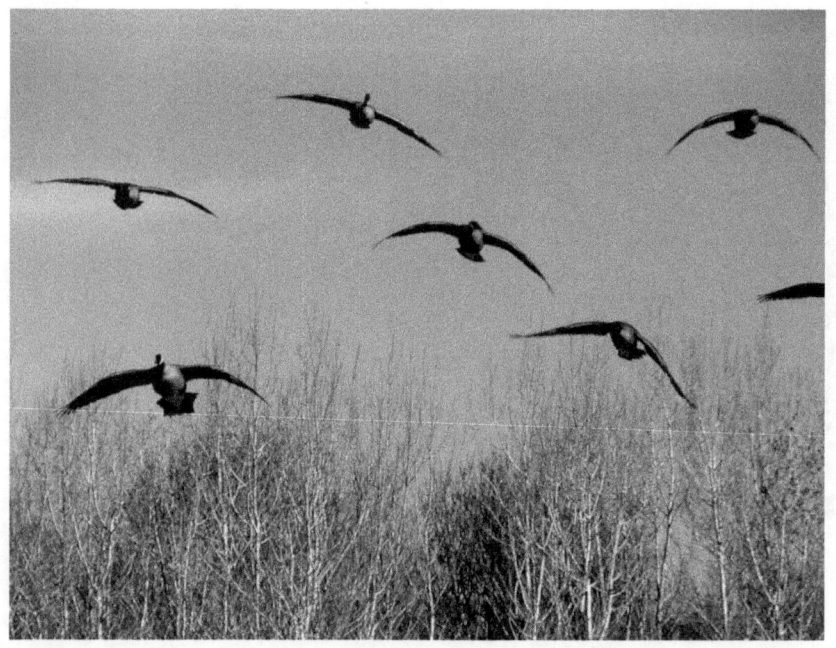

The pattern here was the geese. The picture above of the
pond I shot in infrared, the one with the trees sticking out
of it. The city was trying to kill off the invasive weeds in
the pond, so they drained all the water out of it. I was
standing about 100 yard out in the pond that dried up, and
the geese were coming into land, they landed about 30 feet
in front of me.

Colors

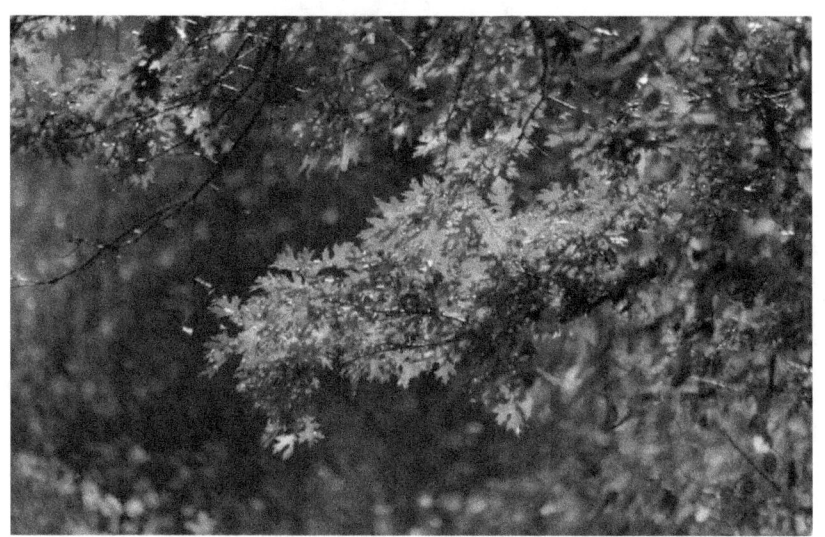

Colors are a fun challenge, pick a color and go out shooting. Look for the color you selected, and try to find that color wherever you are, and make a great picture out of it.

You will surprise yourself at how many places you will see a particular color, where you never even noticed it before.

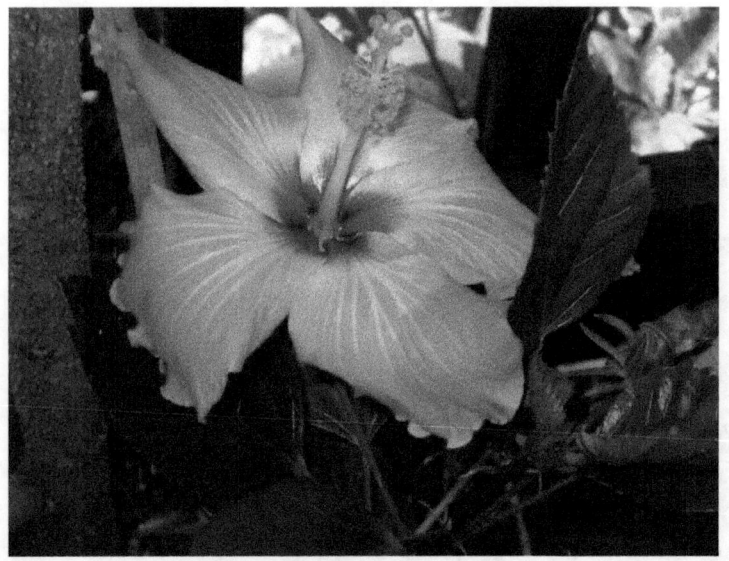

The more vibrant the color you chose, and the more contrasting you can make it in the shot, the more it will stand out and make it look better.

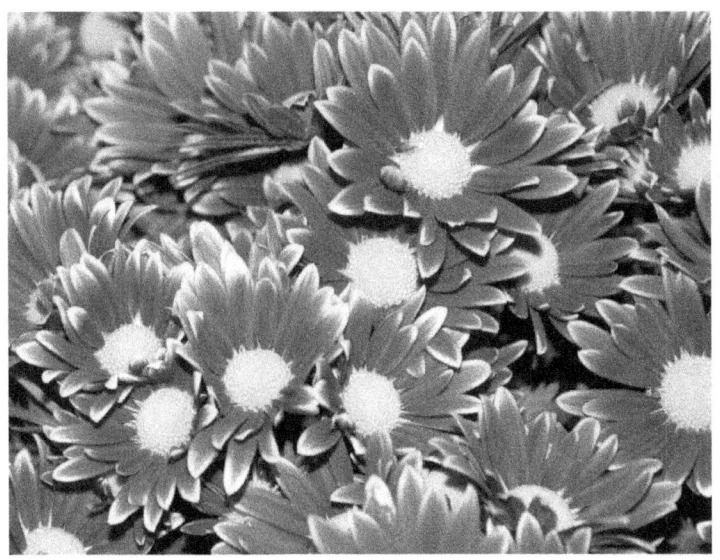

For this shot, my color was yellow. Even though the yellow is not the main color in the shot, it makes the photo pop because of it.

Yellow and purple contrasting colors that make both colors look better.

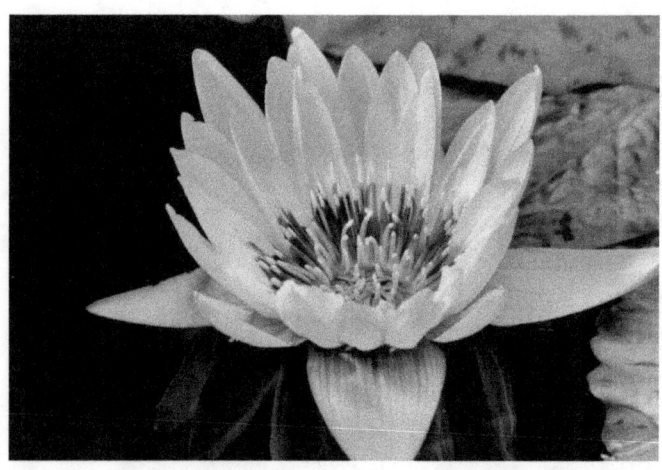

Flowers are one of the best things to look for when you are doing a color challenge.

They do not have to be the focus of the shot; the colors can add to the shot to make it better.

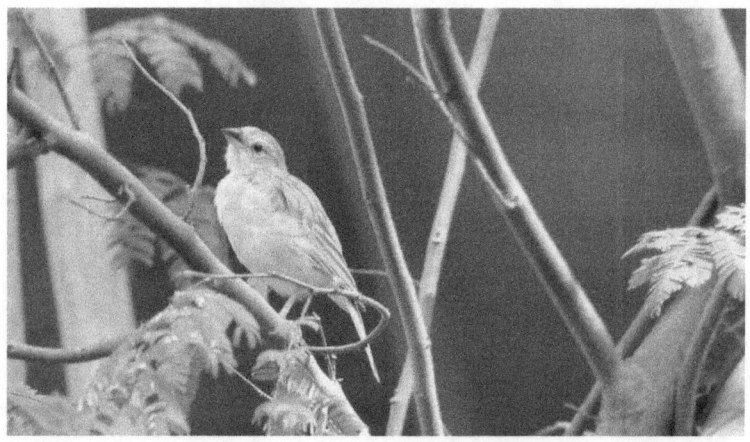

Another yellow color picks. The green of the leaves and
the various grey shades of the tree trunk, all add the yellow
by making it stand out more.

Framing your shot

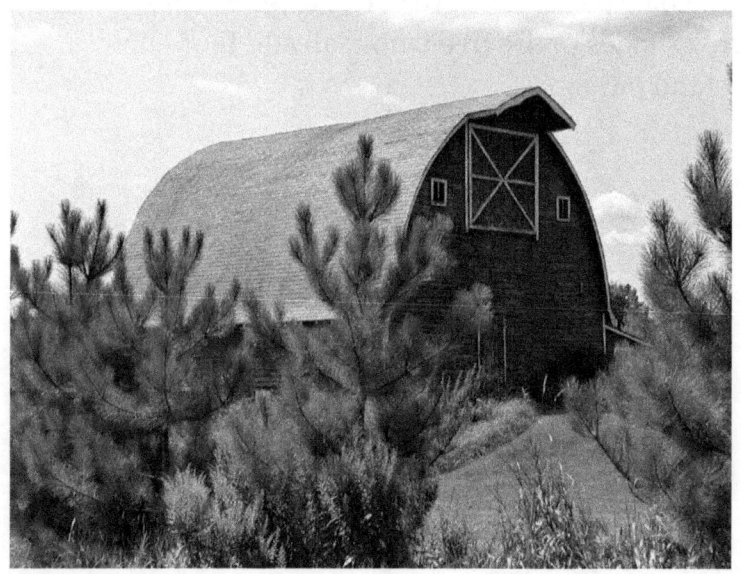

Framing is something I try to do on a large percentage of the landscape shots I take. You can frame it on top and bottom, or on the sides, or both. This shot I used the pine trees to frame the top of the barn.

You can also use the side of the picture as a framing element combined with a natural frame.

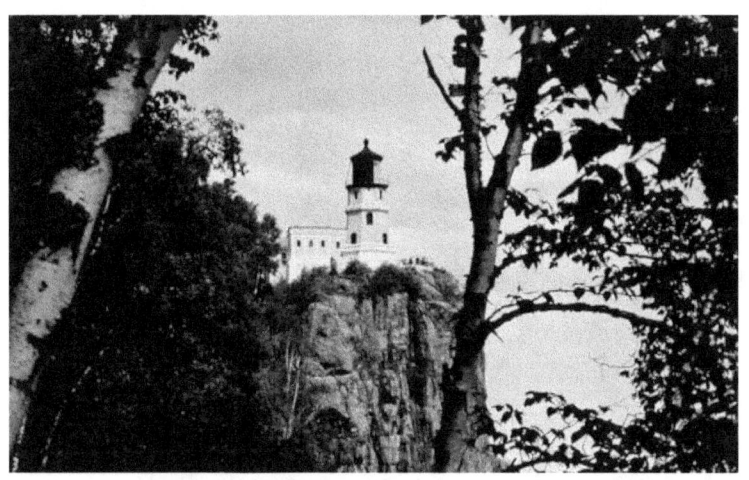

This is a fun shot I took at Split rock lighthouse on the North shore of Lake Superior. I saw the spot to frame the shot between the birch trees and it felt like it worked.

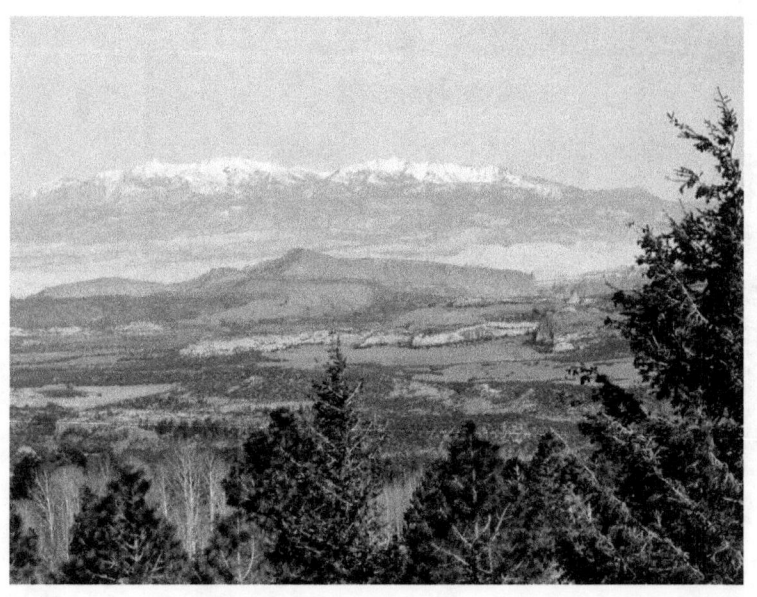

Sometimes you can make great landscape shots with a long zoom. The ability to compress the distance adds a lot to this shot. The trees in the foreground are a decent way in front of where I was standing. I kept the focus to get the full effect of the color in the mid part of the shot, then added the snow covered peak across the valley. Putting it all together because it worked well for the full shot.

The peaks on the far side of the valley are over 80 miles away from where I am standing. It is one of my favorite places. Just north of Bryce Canyon National Park in central Utah.

The shot below is a statue in Como Park in St Paul Minnesota, framed between two trees.

The key to most framing is the get the subject and the frame in focus although sometimes it works well to have the frame blurred so it is not in focus.

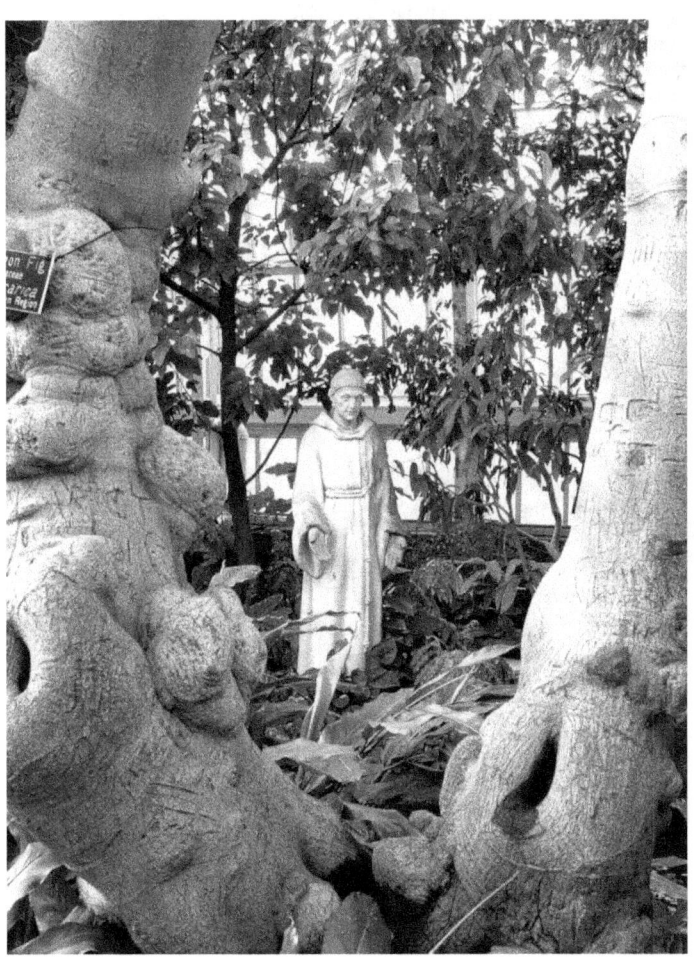

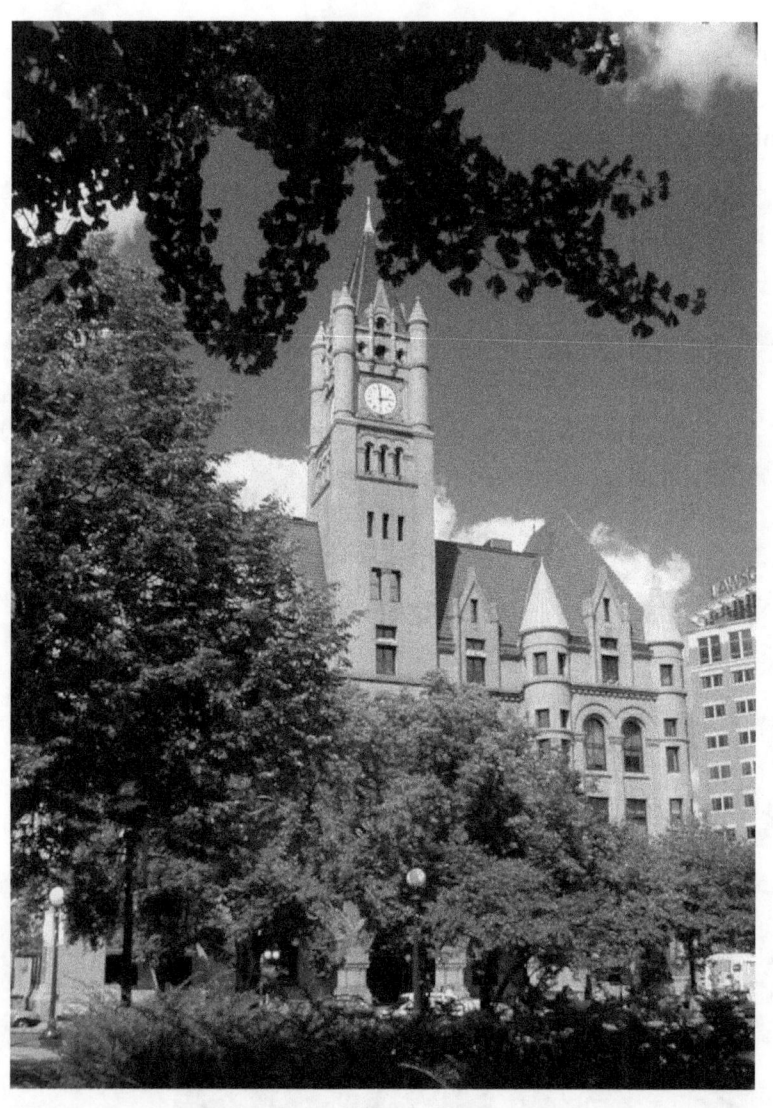

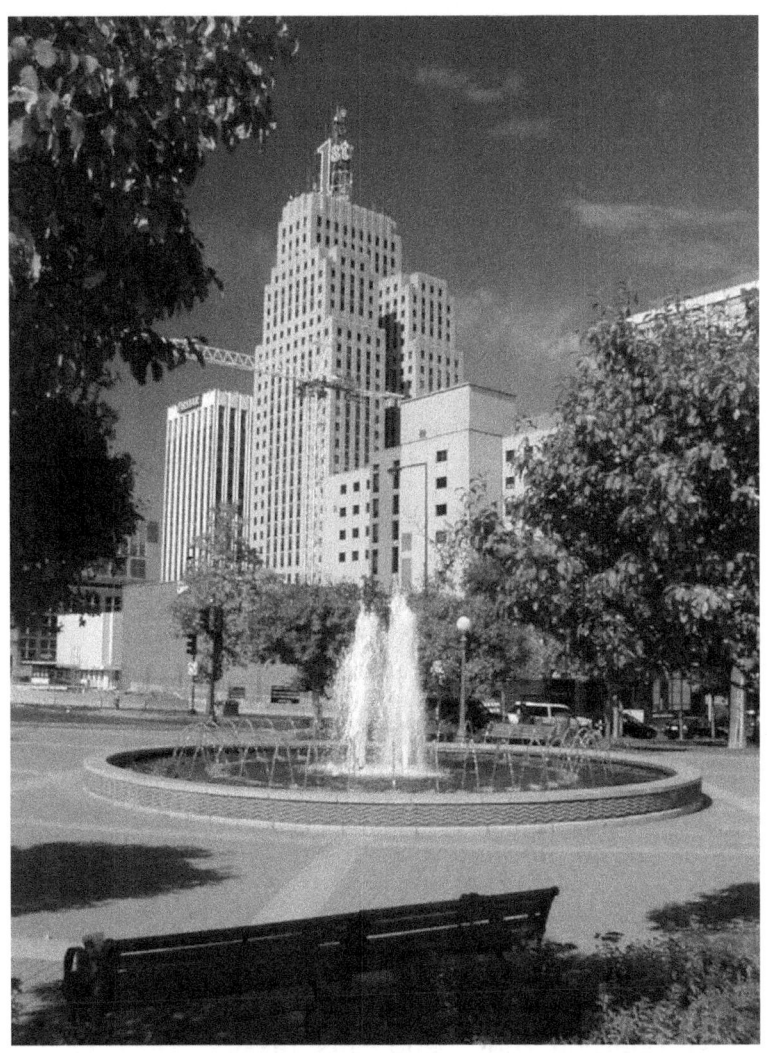

The two shots above are nice, framed shots of buildings I used tree branches as the frame to draw attention to the buildings as the main subject.

Conclusion

The whole reason to do projects is to get yourself to see things you would not see, by forcing you to look at things more intently. Our lives are so busy now days we miss a lot of what is around us, even if we see it every day.

Making yourself slow down and look at things and seeing every part of the things we look at; will make you advance ahead in your photography by huge strides.

Being able to see things and being able to make the photo composition interesting and cool, will make you a much better photographer.

Going from someone who takes snapshots, to becoming someone who makes pictures is something that, like anything else takes practice. Just taking lots of pictures will not make you a better photographer if you are not learning as you go.

There are more people taking pictures than ever before. A cell phone with a real camera has made everyone a potential photographer, but most people just take snapshots of things, and never think about what they are looking at, or composing the shot to make it better.

Learn to look and learn to see these things, and you will become a good or great photographer, even if you do not have the top-of-the-line equipment, you can still make great photos.

Thank you for reading my book. If you have a minute, I would appreciate if you would go to the Amazon website and write a short review of the book so other people will see your review and want to read the book so they can also become a better photographer.

Also, if you are interested, check out my other books.

Black and white photography the art of making great black and white photos

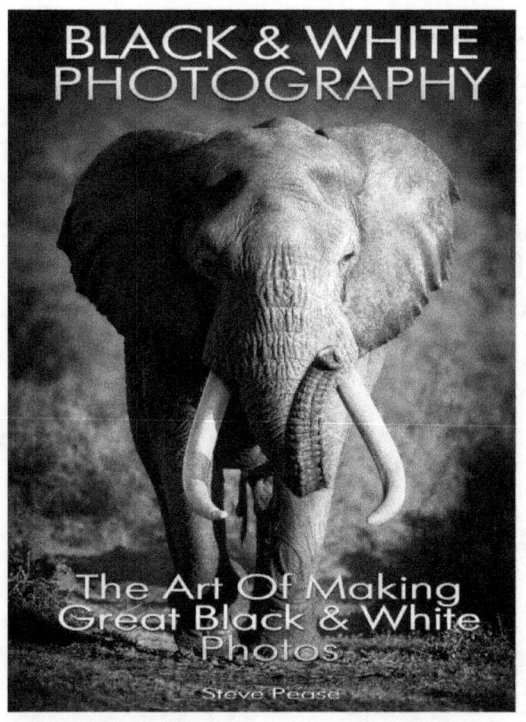

How to take great photos with your phone and tablet. Tips to make you a great photographer.

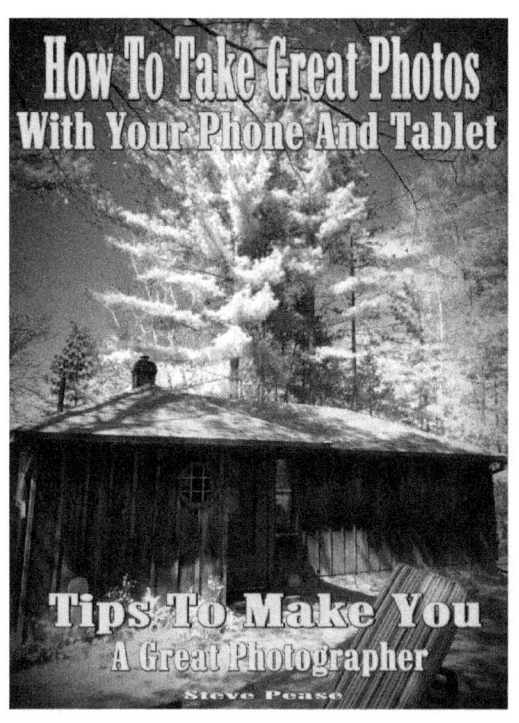

Portrait photography. Tips for taking great people shots.

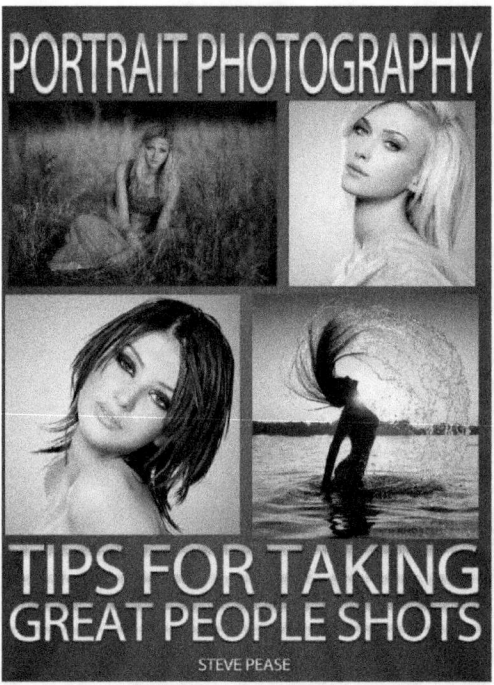

PORTRAIT PHOTOGRAPHY

TIPS FOR TAKING
GREAT PEOPLE SHOTS

STEVE PEASE

www.ingramcontent.com/pod-product-compliance
Lightning Source LLC
Chambersburg PA
CBHW051919170526
45168CB00001B/460